Igbo Philosophy Of Law

By

F.U. Okafor,
B.A. (Hons) M.A., Ph.D., P.G. Dip. Ed.

Department of Philosophy
University of Nigeria, Nsukka

i

Published 1992 by
Fourth Dimension Publishing Co. Ltd.
Plot 64A City Layout. P.M.B.01164, New Haven
Enugu, Nigeria

© 1992 Okafor

ISBN 978 156 134 3 Pb
978 156 192 0 Hc

CONDITIONS OF SALE

"The bird has an honor that man does not have. Man lives in the trap of his fabricated laws and traditions; but the birds live according to the natural law of God who causes the earth to turn around the sun".

K. Gibran

Acknowledgment

I wish to gratefully acknowledge all the help that was rendered to me by friends, colleagues and others with whom I came into contact in the process of producing this work. I thank in particular my colleagues at the Faculty of Law, University of Nigeria, Nsukka especially Prof. D.I.O. Ewelukwa who read through the manuscript and offered many useful suggestions. I thank Dr. Obinna Okere for our fruitful discussions on Jurisprudence in relation to this work. I am also grateful to Mrs. I. P. Enemuo for her brilliant notes on Introduction to Nigerian Law which I found very helpful in the course of my research work.

I am highly indebted to the presidents of the Customary Courts, the traditional rulers, elders, and "philosophers" from across the length and breadth of the Igbo land who are too numerous to be mentioned individually. These were invaluable resource persons. I am equally grateful to my colleagues at the Department of Philosophy, University of Nigeria, Nsukka for their collective interest in doing, projecting and encouraging research in African Philosophy in general.

Special mention should be made of Professors, Dario Composta and Francesco Belda. The former first stimulated my interest in Legal Philosophy, the latter nurtured it. I am also profoundly grateful to Professor Victor Uchendu for making available his pioneering work on the Igbo of South-east Nigeria.

Finally, I am grateful to my wife, Vera, and our two children, Chibuzo and Chizoba for providing a peaceful and happy home where I retired into each day of the long and arduous process of writing this book.

iv

Foreword

It gives me a great deal of pleasure to write a foreword to this interesting first attempt at the philosophical articulation and projection of the Igbo man's conception of law and the role of law in his traditional environment. Social life and cohesion cannot exist without law, for no community can exist or even come into being without a system of social/legal controls; community life, sentiments and cohesion can emerge and survive only within the framework of a legal order. This book, *Igbo Philosophy of Law*, clearly shows that the traditional Igbo republics had their own peculiar ideas of law and legal rights, for none of them existed outside the pale of law. Their legal system consisted of a set of norms which slowly crystallised from their time-honoured usages and institutions and those which were consciously enacted. The author is definitely not one of the theorists with extreme and outlandish ideas of law, who argue that law consists of only formally enacted and recorded norms and should never include customs whose observance is required and enforced by recognized authorities in non-literate societies. Written by a lecturer in philosophy, the book is sure to stir a lively interest in Igbo man's conception of law and morality.

The author has in the book carefully articulated and lucidly explained what, in his view, are the Igbo man's ideas of the true nature of law, underlining clearly the relationship between positive law, natural law, divine law and moral law in Igboland. He shows that, among the Igbos, positive law, morality and religion are so linked up that a breach of positive law offends not only human beings living and dead, but God (*Chi-Ukwu*) as well. Therefore, the trial of the case may begin in a human court (say, *Umunna*) and end up finally in a judicial forum provided by the traditional religion in the form of oath-taking. Oath taking was so widely accepted and respected among the Igbos that it was adopted with some minor modifications, first, by the colonial administrators and, then, by the leaders of the Christian religion.

It is quite interesting to note from the book that the legislative process of the traditional Igbo republics was far more democratic and reassuring than what we now have under the modern constitutional system. The process was a kind of filter that removed from a legislative proposal all human factors and objectionable features that could make it unreasonable, unfair and unjust. Every family and, in fact, every adult had a say in the making of law, and every enacted law must go through some ratification ritual designed to secure for it the blessings of the people and gods. Therefore, laws usually were general in operation and cut across individual and sectional interests; they were aimed at the evils of the day and sought to promote justice, welfare and common good of all. They were supposed to regulate men's behaviour so as to qualify them for the ultimate spiritual goal of sharing in the happy reunion with their ancestors in the life after death. Such laws were therefore happily obeyed, not because policemen and law enforcement agencies were standing by to punish offenders, but because they were in conformity with the wishes and desires of the people, their ancestors and God, and any violation of them might constitute an abomination (*Nsoani*) which if not cleansed would surely disqualify a person from joining in the happy reunion hereafter.

Lawyers are in the habit of studying and practising or teaching law without ever pausing to consider or understand what law means to the common man in the small community in which he lives. This publication by a lecturer in philosophy constitutes a challenge to lawyers to join in the quest for the true meaning of law to the past and present generations of the various ethnic groups in the country.

D.I.O. Ewelukwa
Professor of Law,
University of Nigeria,
Enugu campus, Enugu.

Preface

Law is both a divine and human institution. The immutable laws that regulate the course of the universe are certainly of divine origin. These laws are universally binding on all creatures, across space and time. Human laws are but expressions of the eternal laws. Laws made by man, therefore, should primarily be established on the immutable principles of natural laws; natural laws understood as divine laws as applying to man *qua* moral being, in which sense, they could be referred to as moral laws; and as applying to other creatures in so far as they form part of divine plan.

Human positive laws must therefore first and foremost have regard for the noble end and destiny of man. This is to say that human laws should be means to an end and not end *per se*. But experience has shown that many human positive laws are devoid of these teleological and moral considerations. Laws and legal systems that are borne of erroneous and defective philosophical doctrines are bound to be deficient in part or whole and are likely to be detrimental to the societies where they apply.

Conscious, therefore, of the need for a sound concept of law as bulwark against inhuman and unjust laws, convinced of the general and particular impacts of each legal system or body of laws on the particular society in which they obtain and conversant with the relationship between law and right, I have addressed myself to a fundamental, and philosophical inquiry into the nature of law and right in the traditional society of the Igbo of Nigeria.

Long before the advent of western civilization and the consequent adoption of western legal system and laws in Igbo land and other parts of Nigeria, the Igbo had their own legal system and body of laws. Though the Igbo concept of law is not systematised, various categories of law can be identified. The Igbo clearly distinguish between the laws made by man - human positive laws and, laws evident in nature - natural laws. The concepts of divine laws and .moral laws are also discernible in Igbo traditional thought. But whereas in western societies numerous works on philosophy of law have been produced over the centuries, African societies lack such written accounts. The Igbo society is no exception. In writing therefore, on the nature of law and right in Igbo society, my method will be deductive.

This work aims at escavating the basic concepts of law in Igboland. It will examine the various types of laws and attempts to categorise them. Furthermore, it will consider the essential elements of Igbo positive laws and the ends of laws in Igbo society. Finally, because of the inter-dependence of law and right, the notion of rights will be duly examined and systematised.

The work will consist of three parts. The First or Introductory Part will be descriptive and is intended to give the reader an insight into the moral, religious, socio-political and legal background of the Igbo. The Second Part will be devoted to the fundamental questions concerning the concept of law, the various types of laws, the reciprocal influence between law and Igbo religion and the end of laws, all these as they are found in the streams of Igbo traditional thoughts. The Third and the last part will be concerned with an examination of the nature of right in Igbo traditional thought and locating the philosophical background against which rights are believed by the Igbo to be a human natural property.

In conclusion, I will critically assess the merits of the Igbo indigenous legal phenomena with an eye on the demerits of legal positivism.

O.U.F.

Introduction

Many praiseworthy research works on the Igbo people are already in circulation. Many more interesting books on the Igbo have been written by Igbo and non-Igbo scholars. The result is a rich harvest of information about the people. But these research works on the Igbo people were mainly conducted by Anthropologists, Sociologists and Historians who were solely concerned with the social structure, political organisation, culture, religion and the historical evolution of the Igbo. A more profound and more fundamental aspect is therefore left uncovered - the philosophical aspect.

Few writers on the Igbo people have ventured to study the Igbo institutions and life from a philosophical perspective. The few who realised the indispensability of the knowledge of the fundamental Igbo concepts of the physical and the metaphysical in understanding the Igbo and the totality of their world made only a brief commentary on the concepts as introduction to their work. Perhaps, the reason why so little interest has been shown in this aspect of the Igbo world is the paucity of indigenous philosophers - something indeed regrettable.

In this work, I undertake a philosophical inquiry into one vital Igbo institution - Law and its corollary, Rights. I choose the Igbo traditional law as a subject of my philosophical research because law is essential in all societies and it covers practically all aspects of human existence.

The raw materials for this singular understating will come from what is already written about the Igbo people. I will therefore draw largely from the wealth of research already conducted by others and all relevant available written works on the Igbo. These will supplement my own personal research.

My method will be deductive. This means that out of general observations, particular conclusions will be made. Of course, this has to be so for the work not only tries to discover the basic concepts of law in Igbo traditional society but also attempts to analyse these concepts and place them in their appropriate philosophical compartments. Therefore this is not mere description of Igbo laws.

By Igbo traditional society in this discussion, I mean what is generally called the Igbo village setting. Life and ideas as lived and held in the urban centres are to a large extent different from what obtain in the villages. In spite of the fact that uban style of life and development are rapidly surging into the villages, the typical Igbo villages remain the reservoir of their hoary culture; there much of their original beliefs, customs, world-view and values are to be found. The physical features of these villages are changing fast in the face of modern infrastructures. But in the realm of belief and ideas, the changes are not very rapid.

Admittedly, Western Civilisation has made a considerable impact on some Igbo institutions. A few Igbo institutions have fallen under the weight of their western counter-parts. Others have remained intact and without a western rival while a few others are surviving *vis a vis* their western opposite numbers. This observation has also been made by Njaka. He writes:

> There is a recognised coexistence of Igbo
> and alien political systems in Igbo land.[1]

The Igbo legal institution is one of such that exists side by side the western or western oriented one. This fact is borne out by the existence of customary courts, set up by the British Colonial Authorities, organised along western pattern, to which cases of purely traditional nature are referred. That the British Authorities had to create customary courts is a clear demonstration of their recognition of the importance and the role of Igbo Native Laws and Customs in maintaining social harmony and cohesion.

The customary courts are not however substitutes for the Igbo traditional "Forum" for settling dispute. Uptill today, conflicts between individuals in the villages, offenders in law etc are brought before the appropriate traditional tribune. In fact, in many villages in Igbo country of today, laws are made prohibiting members of the community from taking cases to the customary courts or magistrate courts except such cases that could not be settled in the traditional ways about which I shall speak shortly. The effect of cases tried in the customary courts is that they are enforceable by means of official government agents.

Some authorities, in determining what qualifies as law in Igbo traditional society have used enforceability as their ultimate criterion. Clearly not every rule qualifies as law in Igbo society but we must employ other criteria in determining those that are laws and those that are mere "customary rules".

It has to be noted that Igbo laws and customs are so closely knit together that one cuts into the other. I shall regard as laws the whole body of rules, customary, legal, conventional, ethical, which pass the tests of a law and are so regarded in the Igbo community.

---

[1] Njaka, E.N., *Igbo Political Culture*, Evanton, Northwestern University Press, 1974. p.

Content

Chapter 1

Igbo Socio-Political Set-Up

Every society is made up of growing number of individual families. In a typical Igbo family, much of what should be known about the life and organisation of an Igbo man is transparent. I shall therefore first discuss a typical Igbo family.

Igbo Family

In the context of Igbo traditional society, the word "family" has a much wider meaning than it has in western societies. Whereas A.S. Hornby gave a simple dictionary definition of family in western usage as "parents and children", this definition is far from being functional in Igbo usage. In Igbo communities, there are no vernacular terms which denote the various categories and depth of social groups unlike in western societies where such terms abound. This fact make a working definition of a family in Igbo context even more difficult.

Taking many factors into consideration, the definition of family in Nigeria context given by Obi is quite functional.

According to him:

> The primary meaning of 'family' as used in Nigeria is a social institution consisting of all persons who are descended through the same line (the male line in a patrilineal, the female line in a matrilineal society) from a common ancestor, and who still owe allegiance to or recognise the over-all authority of one of their number as head and legal successor to the said ancestral founder, together with any persons who though not blood descendants of the founder, are for some reason attached to the households of persons so descended, or have otherwise been absorbed into the lineage as a whole.[1]

This is in fact the primary meaning of the word family in Igboland in particular for this is what comes to mind when the word family is mentioned.

The secondary meaning of the word family in Igbo context is a social unit comprising a man and his wife or wives with their unmarried children and any other dependants such as wards and domestic servants. If we call this

---

[1] Obi, S.N.C., *Modern Family Law in Southern Nigeria*, London, Sweet and Maxwell, 1966, p. 9.

"elementary" family, we have to bear in mind that in Igbo society, the "elementary" family, in the case of polygamous family, may be composed of two or more sub-divisions or branches corresponding to the number of women by whom the father of the family has had children. Furthermore, it is legitimate in some parts of Igboland for one's unmarried daughter to raise issues in her father's house. In such a case the children are part of the man's elementary family. So whether in its primary or secondary sense, the composition and the organisation of Igbo family is complex. In what follows, family is to be understood in the primary sense.

Structure And Organisation

In the traditional Igbo society, each family is made up of territorially kin-based units called *Umunna*. The family is made up of a number of compounds. The compound called *Ezi* or *Obi* in vernacular consists of a number of economically independent household each with a man or woman as a householder. A "big compound" is an ideal one - one consisting of a large number of households.

A high degree of harmony and order is achieved through the respected "office" of the compound head. All the householders and their dependants recognise the full authority of the compound head and are expected to consult him before taking a major political decision. *Onye nwe ezi (obi)* as the compound head is addressed in some parts of Igboland has numerous ritual, moral and legal rights and obligations. He offers sacrifice for the welfare of his compound members, whom he helps to extricate from their ritual, social and legal difficulties; he settles matrimonial cases and confers a special name on each child born in his compound. In Igbo idiom, he is the "eyes" of his compound members as they are his "ears". He represents them in their external dealings with other like social groups. Any injury inflicted on any member of his groups without his having first been notified is considered a personal injury for which he makes a personal reprisal if need be.

In effect, a strong compound head in a shield of protection and the wall or fence surrounding his compound is his group's castle.[2]

Such is the authority of the head of the compound, an authority exercised in true spirit of democracy. For though his authority is recognised by every household in the compound, he does not interfere in their internal affairs. He does not normally initiate political action either, but is always

---

[2] Uchendu, V.C., *The Igbo Southeast Nigeria*, New York, Holt, Rinehart and Winston, 1965, p. 40.

aware of what action is planned, for he must give his opinion on their conflict with custom and tradition. He is in a word, a counsellor; respected and not feared. He is invested with a power to punish by only one sanction: "cursing people on his *Ọfọ* - a sanction oftened threatened but seldom invoked".[3]

The family head in turn is entitled to periodic tributes and gifts in kind from other members of the family. This is not however a legal entitlement. Succession to the office of the head of the family follows the line of primogeniture. At the death of the family head, the oldest member of the family automatically takes his position.

In the secondary sense of the word, it is a social imperative for a man to raise his own family. In fact, if a young man waits too long before he marries, he is regarded as an *Okalioholi* a useless vagabond. "Polygamy, a symbol of high social status, is the ideal".[4]

Igbo marriage is an alliance between two families rather than a contract between two individuals. It establishes a new social link not only between families but also between the villages of the bride and the bridegroom. In the words of M.M. Green:

> Inter-marriage creates a network of ties by which the cells of Ibo society, though not united by any central government authority, nor arranged in any political hierarchy, are nonetheless interlinked horizontally each with its neigbours by the social bonds of inter-marriage.[5]

Children are regarded as direct blessing from God. In Igboland, the end of marriage is procreation. Childless marriage is therefore a tragic failure. And to live and die without raising issue is one of the most abysmal tragedies that can befall an Igboman. Marriage and procreation are thus inseparably conceived as one entity.

The husband-wife relationship is not that of a master and slave as some foreign writers on Igbo family wrongly held. Basden, for instance wrote that:

> A wife ordinarily has no rights, either over herself or her possessions, not including her children. She is part and parcel of her husband's property .[6]

---

3 Uchendu, V.C., *op. cit*. p. 41.

4 Uchendu, V.C., op. cit, p. 49

5 Green, M.M., *Ibo Village Affairs*, New York, Frederick A. Praeger, Publishers, 2nd ed., 1964, p. 8.

6 Basden, G.T., *Among the Ibos of Nigeria*, London, 1966, 2nd ed., p. 32.

This is at best an exaggeration. The husband does not treat his wife as a mere property in Igbo community. He rather exercises great caution not to injure his wife's feelings.

According to Green:

> If a woman's husband neglects her or treats her badly she may return to her parents' home... A woman may also, if she is annoyed or offended, slip out of her husband's home and back to her native place for a day or two.[7]

When this happens, the husband is expected usually to take a conciliatory gift to her father-in-law to beg the woman to return. Even in the management of family affairs, the wife has a considerable say. Writing on his subject, Anochie observes that:

> In the traditional society, men, after carefully testing the wisdom and discretion of their wives, do not hesitate to lay their problems before them to share in their thoughts and to a certain extent guide their activities [8]

The phrase, "after carefully testing the wisdom and discretion of their wives" is important because there is a general diffidence in women in Ibo country. There is a saying in my locality that *Onye ji nwayi bulu ibu bu isi nkiti* (whoever has woman supporter is alone).[x]

In public matters however, women have not much say. But by means of various kinds of women's organisation or groups, their opinion and their impact are felt in village affairs.

Such is the structure and organisation of Igbo family. We shall see the position and the role of the family in the overall socio-political set-up.

Igbo System Of Government

The British Colonial Administration encountered obstacles of great magnitude when it first came to Igboland. It had enjoyed considerable success in the western and northern parts of Nigeria. Through the agencies of the western Obas and northern Emirs, the British Authorities successfully introduced a system of indirect rule in those areas.

---

[7] Green, M.M., *op. cit.* p. 164.

[8] Anochie, R.C., *The Impact of Igbo Women on The Church in Igboland*, Rome, Tip. Centanari, 1979, p. 26.

[x] Trans. by the author.

Failing to find powerful chiefs who wielded influence over a large territory, as were found in the northern and western parts of Nigeria, they naively concluded that the Igbo were living in 'ordered anarchy.[9]

But the Igbo were infact living in 'sane democracy'. A British social Anthropologist, M.M. Green, writing on Igbo village affairs pointed out:

> That there is political organisation, on the other hand, in the sense that the ends of government are to some extent secured, is an undoubted fact.[10]

The Igbo political institutions and machinery, we shall now proceed to examine.

The political institutions in Igboland differ in their structure. Some of these, like the kingship institutions of Onitsha, Nri and Aguleri are intrusive traits. Although age-grade associations, title-making societies, *Dibia* fraternities (medicine men), secret societies and oracles are among the traditional instruments of government, the role of each in the political processes of a given village-group differs markedly. Nevertheless, there emerges a general pattern of political process which is shared by all Igbo.

The concept of central government and central authority is alien to Igbo political system.

> Anything of the nature of the sovereign state, which has so largely dominated the political consciousness of Europe since the Reformation, is in conception and in fact absent in this part of Africa. Power politics appear also to be absent.[11]

Now, two main layers of political structure are clearly identifiable: the village and the village-group. Political activities revolve around these two social units. It is important here to note the difference between a 'village' and a 'village-group'. A village is a social unit comprising the lineages; a village-group is a agglomeration of individual villages to form a broad political community. The name 'town' is sometimes used, particularly in official reports to describe social units of this kind, but the designation "village group" is to be preferred. Government at the village level is by direct democracy and the system is still in vogue today.

A representative system of government is adopted at the village-group level. This is made workable through the principle of equality among the associating villages and through the principle of equal "sharing of kola" and equal contribution of material resources for the upkeep of the community.

---

[9] Uchendu, V.C., *op. cit.* p. 46.

[10] Green, M.M., *op. cit.* p. 5.

[11] Green, M.M., *op. cit.* p. 9.

The institutions which are part and parcel of the political organisation include *Amala, Oha* (a general assembly), the title-making societies, the *Dibia* fraternity (a priestly association), the secret society (*Manwu*), oracles and the age-grade associations. The role of each one of these institutions will emerge clearly as we discuss the legislative, the judiciary and the executive arms of Igbo traditional government.

The Legislative Procedure

The Igbo do not have a permanent legislative body or assembly nor a legislative house as is known in the western world. M.M. Green writes:

> There seems to be no specialised institution for this function and one meets again the fact that a group of people met together for some economic purpose such as a market or some traditional purpose such as a second burial will use the occasion of meeting to discuss public matters. It is as though the *res publica* were only gradually emerging from the sphere of kingship group, but if specialised institutions are hard to discover, this is not to say that the Igbo do not make and proclaim laws - *iti iwu*.[12]

Generally, all adults males meeting in ad hoc general assembly called *Oha* have full rights to participate in the legislative activities. As we have noted earlier on, there is no special forum for such meetings. However, when and where they take place, opportunity is usually seized to discuss public matters, including the making of laws. Everybody who has an opinion on the issue being discussed is given a hearing. When all possible views have been expressed, the heads from each lineage in the village retire for a 'close session'. The right to participate in this close or better 'consultative session' called *izuzu* is reserved to men of high regard with sufficient wisdom to discern the direction of public opinion. At the end of *izuzu* session, a spokesman, usually an eloquent fellow from the group announces the decision. This final decision is either accepted by the general assembly which acceptance is usually expressed by a general acclamation or rejected by shouts of disapproval. Invariably, the view and will of the assemble prevail. For according to V.C. Uchendu:

> The Igbo are jealous of their legislative authority and are unwilling to surrender to a small group of individuals.[13]

In some cases however, issues of public interest would be considered by an independent group such as age-grade association, *Dibia* fraternity, council of

---

[12] Green, M.M., *op. cit.* p. 152

[13] Uchendu, V.C., *op. cit.* p. 42.

elders, titled-men, privately and then brought to public notice for further deliberation. Sometimes, the matter so presented could win public approval and thus acquires the force of law. In either case, the will of the people expressed by the *Oha* is final. Any of the groups mentioned above could initiate a legislative move but cannot impose any law on the people.

Once a decision has been thus acclaimed into law, it is given a ritual binder by the *Ọfọ* holders, who invoke this formula: "This *iwu* (law) is in accordance with our custom and must be obeyed and respected. Those who refuse to obey the law, may *Ọfọ* kill them". Each time the *Ọfọ* is struck on the ground (usually four times), the assembly assents with *iha* or *ise* (let it be so). This done, it becomes the duty of each male adult and householders to explain the legislation to his household group and to see to it that the members respect the law. Writing on the legislative procedure adumbrated above, M.M. Green states:

> One had the impression again that laws only establish themselves by degrees and then only in so far as they gain general acceptance. A law does not either exist or not: rather it goes through a process of establishing itself by common consent or of being shelved by a series of quiet evasions. The law *in posse* may or may not become the law *in esse*. [14]

Laws are made on wide range of subjects including economic, social and political matters. New laws are made as the need arises and the existing laws subject to amendment if need be. One basic fact emerges from the foregoing - that the legislative power rests with the people, the *Oha*.

The Judicial Methods

There is no specialised courts as such entrusted with judicial matters. Judicial methods may at times appear informal, but they follow recognised if diverse line. However, there are known institutions to which judicial matters could be referred. These include the age-grade society, the *Dibia* fraternity, societies of titled fellows, village-elders and the *okonko* or *manwu* society. Others are supernatural tribunes to which offences of grave nature or judicial matters which cannot be resolved by the ordinary judicial procedures are referred.

There are two main classes of offences: offences which are *nso* (abomination) and those which are not. This classification of offence is very important in Igbo society. As Green puts it:

---

[14] Green, M.M., *op. cit.* p. 137

Legal rules are of two main classes and are recognised as such. There are those which might be called ordinary human laws and those whose breach is held to be not only illegal but also offence against a supernatural power particularly *Ala*, the land. Of the perpetrator of such an offence it would be said: *Omeruru ala* - he polluted the land. Such offences are usually said to be *nso* - taboo - and are distinguished from merely natural offences.[15]

I shall examine, first, offences which are not *nso* and the judicial processes any offender may undergo or what legal action the offended party may take.

A classical offence that comes to mind is theft. The judicial treatment of a thief may vary with the nature of the theft but the offence is generally regarded as serious in Igbo community.

If a man steals from a kinsman, the victim will summon the kinsmen and report the culprit to them. The thief will receive serious warning besides being rigorously rebuked if what was stolen is a trifle. Otherwise, the offender is tied up for days without food; if caught red-handed he is carried about the village with the stolen property conspicuously exhibited, while passers-by curse, ridicule, and spit on him. Stealing from outsiders is even more serious for the thief is held until a substantial ransom is paid by his relatives. In former times, if the ransom is not paid the culprit is sold into slavery.

Before any of the actions specified above is taken against the thief, there must be substantial evidence that he is guilty of the offence. False accusation is equally grave and care is taken to avoid it. This is why if the thief is not actually caught and the evidence against a suspect is not convincing, the suspect is made to swear to an oath. If he swears his oath and no bad luck befalls him within one year, his innocence is regarded as proved and he celebrates it appropriately. So far we have been discussing a case of theft in which the offender owned up his guilt and received a standard punishment.

In other cases of offence in law, the injured party or parties, seeking justice, have a number of courses open to them. So too are parties in legal dispute. The injured party, taking the initiative may first appeal to the head of the compound (house-group) of the offender or to a body of arbitrators depending on the nature of the dispute or case. Since the arbitrators are not a legally constituted body (for the Igbo have no specialized courts), they cannot enforce their decision. Extra effort is therefore needed to arrive at a decision which will be acceptable to both parties. If this fails, the injured party may summon the *Amala*, a higher body than the former. Close friends

---

[15] Green, M.M., *op. cit.* p. 99

of the litigant are asked to participate. At this stage, the issue may be resolved but if not further appeals may be made by the injured party. Other institutions which may be appealed to for judicial opinion include the age-grade association, the *Dibia* fraternity, various title-making societies and the *okonko* or *manwu* society. It has been observed earlier on that judicial methods are informal and, in fact follow diverse lines.

When all these recognised judicial fora have failed to resolve the issue to the satisfaction of both parties, appeal is made to a supernatural tribune which is the "last court of appeal". This appeal to the supernatural tribune takes the form of swearing. The accused may swear his innocence upon invoking a powerful oracle. If property is the object of legal dispute, one of the parties is made to swear that the property in question is his. The oath being thus sworn, the injured party is satisfied to regard the accused innocent or in the case of property, to relinquish the property to the swearer. If after a period of time, the swearer meets no bad luck, his innocence is thus proved and he rejoices with his relatives. This is the nature of legal proceedings in a typical Igbo community.

The Executive Machinery

It has already been noted that the *oha* the village assembly is an all-purpose body. On it rest the legal, judicial and executive powers. This is why Njaka, an Igbo political scientist has named the Igbo system of government, "*Ohacracy*"; *Ohacracy* is an anglicised Igbo term coined by the combination of "oha" (Igbo term for general assembly) and the prefix - "cracy". (Njaka maintained that:

> *Ohacracy* is preferred here because it retains the African meaning attached to the people as sovereign, and any attempt to translate it would weaken or distort the meaning.[16]

But as the general village assembly cannot in practice be involved in executive details, there arises a need for a delegation of power. Thus the executive function of the village is vested in the youth through their age-grade organisation. Besides serving as a social indicator which separates the seniors from the juniors, the age-grade association is a means of allocating public duties, guarding public morality through the censorship of members' behaviour, and providing companionship and mutual insurance of members. It is to them that the police functions of the village are delegated.

---

[16] Njaka, E. N., *Igbo Political Culture*, Evanston, Northwestern University Press, 1974, p. 13.

The age-grade association is indeed a very powerful executive instrument in Igbo society. Every age-grade association has a code of conduct and a constitution.

Many disciplinary measures are taken to ensure that members adhere to the rules and regulations of the association. It is on account of this high degree of discipline evident in the age-grade association as well as the fact that the association is made up of youths of diverse physical strength and fitness that the executive function of the community is invested on it.

If the village general assembly has decreed that every male adult shall pay certain sum of money into the village treasury, it is usually an age-grade association that is detailed to collect the levies from people who fail to pay up after a fixed date. The age-grade in their executive function is empowered to use force when necessary. The Anthropologist Nzimiro, who made a research on the government of four Igbo village-groups of Onitsha, Oguta, Osomari and Abo wrote:

> In all four states, age sets are used not only for the enforcement of judicial decisions, but also for the recruitment of personnel for the defence of the state. They perform both police and military functions.[17]

The age-grade association also acts as a broker of public work. If a piece of work involves the entire community, the age-grade associations besides playing most active role in the work, perform a supervisory role. Here again, it is their duty to note the absentees and to ensure that appropriate fines are collected from them. It has to be remarked that there is a healthy competition among the various age-grades especially in places of public work. This spirit of progressive competition is responsible for the many social facilities provided by the age-grade associations.

Even nowadays the age-grade associations have continued to play this executive role in the community. They still collect levies, keep surveillance over the property of the village and run its errands.

The government on village level and that of village-group (town) is much the same except that whereas that of village government is based on direct democracy, the government of the village-group involves a representative principle. The village-group government has no wide powers. In fact, it has no well-defined powers except on matters affecting the earthgoddess and the common market-places. What laws or decisions it makes are not binding on any village which is not represented or which disagrees with others. The power of the village is based not on the

---

17 Nzimiro, I., *Studies in Igbo Political Systems, Chieftaincy and Politics in Four Niger States*, University of California Press, 1972, p. 128.

possession of a standing or ad hoc army, nor any admitted right to use coercion, but rather on the consensus of the villages. In the village-group assembly, every village has equal voice. There is no majority decision. There must be unanimous agreement on every occasion. Matters concerning the village-groups (town) are not treated with equal excitement as those affecting the villages.

In recent years, people are growing out of the village mentality and the village-group has risen in importance. Everywhere, nowadays, one hears about various "town" development projects. The emphasis has thus shifted from the village to the village-group.

What we have seen so far is the general pattern of Igbo governments. However, there are very few systems which more or less deviate from this general pattern. We shall examine this briefly.

Monarchical Government In Igboland

The three age-long monarchical institutions in Igboland are to be found in Onitsha, Nri and Aguleri. For our purpose, we shall examine the constitutional monarchy in Onitsha as our sample. As the Anthropologist Uchendu remarked:

> Constitutional monarchy is intrusive in Igbo land. The Onitsha traditional system of government therefore contrasts with other systems.[18]

Located at the east bank of the River Niger, the Onitsha people claim descent from Chima, an eponymous ancestor and came into their present territory from Benin. Their Village-group consisted of two main divisions - Umuezechima and Ugwunabankpa but they later proliferated into six more villages.

Onitsha government is organised along monarchical structure. The king of Onitsha is known officially and addressed as Obi. He is the head of the government. Next to him in hierarchy is the *Onowu* who is as it were his "prime minister". After them follow the three colleges of titled men collectively called *Ndichie* and comprising *Ndichie Okwa* and *Ndichie Okwa-Aranze*. Each of the colleges has a hierarchy of officials who are *ozo* titled men.

Even in a monarchical government such as that of Onitsha, the ultimate power rest with the *oha* the general assembly. In theory, the government of Onitsha consists of the *Obi* and his *Ndichie Ume*, but in practice, each village has a large measure of local autonomy.

---

[18] Uchendu, V. C., *op. cit.* p. 45.

The rights of the *Obi* and his council are regulated by custom. When they exceed their rights, the offended village boycotts the *Obi's* palace. The fact that the office of the *Obi* is elective and not hereditary is perhaps another testimony that the basic principle of Igbo government is democracy.

In this whole discussion, the picture of the Igbo political community which emerges from these settings is one that is territorially small enough to make direct democracy possible at the village level (a political phenomenon reminiscent of Greek City States) and representative assembly at the village-group level practicable. In short, "It is a government in which the principle of equality is respected; in which the use of force is minimal or absent; and in which there are leaders rather than rulers and political cohesion is achieved by rules rather than by laws and by consensus rather than by dictation.[19]

If the Igbo have not achieved any political structure which can be called federation, a confederacy or a state, they have achieved one which is relatively alien to western political concept. This may be called "*Ohacracy*" a term first used by an Igbo political scientist, Njaka.

Mazi Ojike summarizes the Igbo political system as follows:

> The Igbo are the most decentralized and least bureaucratic in political organisation... The political system is so highly democratized that no one feels that one's freedom is stifled. In all levels of political organisation, the people rule themselves through their duly elected representatives. Since there is no salary for filling political post, corruption is rare... a public office is a social responsibility rather than a privilege.[20]

The social, cultural and political background of the Igbo have been highlighted in this chapter. This must be borne in mind throughout our discussion.

---

[19] Uchendu, V. C., *op. cit.* p. 45.

[20] Mbonu, O., *My Africa*, Garden city, N. Y.: Doubleday, 1946, p. 193.

Chapter 2

Igbo Cosmological And Metaphysical World-View

The concepts of the world, physical and metaphysical, held by a people have vital influence on their attitude to and evaluation of life. It is still a valid psychological doctrine that our actions are precipitated by our mental attitude. So do our cosmological and metaphysical ideas determine the basic notions underlying our cultural, religious and social activities. In fact, these notions necessarily though sometimes covertly shape our behaviour and thus guide our actions. It is therefore expedient at this juncture to have a look at the Igbo concepts of the physical and the metaphysical worlds. I shall examine the former under their cosmology and the latter under metaphysics. Cosmology here is to be understood as a philosophical science which studies the material world as regards to its origin, its character and its ultimate end. It is to be distinguished from metaphysics which is concerned with immaterial realities. I shall discuss only such aspect that have direct bearing on the Igbo way of life.

Igbo Cosmological Concepts

Cosmological Optimism

The Igbo regard the physical world as ontologically good. It is a perfect world in structure and a beautiful world in design. It is a beautiful world whose architect is a subject of admiration and adoration. A traditional Igbo song portrays this concept:

> Oyooyo uwa di ya
> Oyooyo uwa di ya
> Chukwu sere aka
> Uwa agwu.

This can be rendered as:

> Beautiful the world extends
> Beautiful the world extends
> If God withdraws His hands
> Instantly the world must end.

The apparent evil and imperfection in the world are not intrinsic. They are rather the negation of the perfect cosmic order usually caused by the actions of men and of the spirits. A popular Igbo proverb says that "*Madu bu njo ala*" - "man makes the world evil". The Igbo saying that "*uwa ezu oke*"

13

which literally means that the world is imperfect does not imply any imperfection in creation but rather stresses the insatiability of human wants.

This dialogue between an Igbo leader and philosopher and a distinguished foreign visitor who made some disparaging remark about his host country is relevant here:

"Do you say that my country is bad? Can the earth or trees or mud walls speak? How do they offend?".

"No", the visitor answered. "As far as I know they don't".

"Well answered", the philosopher replied. "Never speak badly of my country again. Should any of my people offend you, accuse them directly".[1] This dialogue further portrays the Igbo concept that the world is not evil per se.

Because of his belief in the ontological perfection of his world, any evil or imperfection is regarded as extrinsic. This is why continuous droughts, long periods of famine, epidemic diseases and the like are seen by the Igbo as distabilizing forces whose causes must be ascertained by divination. The concept of cause and effect is thus part and parcel of Igbo analytical process. It has been noted in the previous chapter that certain crimes in the Igbo community are regarded as "*nso*" or "*alu*". Of the perpetrator of such crime, it is said "*omerulu - ala*" that is, he polluted the land. In other words, he has spoilt the good land.

It is a point of fact therefore that the Igbo hold an optimistic view of the world. The world is not evil per se. It is a beautiful world, a perfect world at that. This cosmological optimism enables the Igbo to assert himself in the face of distabilizing and dehumanizing elements in the world and to battle with the evil and imperfection he feels around him fully aware that they are generated from external sources that are set to undermine the peace and perfection of his world. How the Igbo tries to subdue these intruding evils shall be seen later in this chapter.

Igbo Cosmogony

Cosmogony is that branch of Cosmology concerned with the origin of the universe. There are numerous cosmological theories. Each cosmological theory is built up against a given cultural and religious background. There is no well defined Igbo theory about the origin of the world. The Igbo notion about the origin of the world is to be found rather in their folklores and mythologies. Here is one of them:

---

[1] Uchendu, V. C., *op. cit.*, p. 18.

"There was once a very wonderful man. He created the different parts of the body - the Head, Feet, Hands, Eyes, and other members. When he had completed all he placed them in a beautiful garden, he gave them certain laws to observe, the chief of which were that they should be liberal in almsgiving and that they should show kindness and hospitality to all strangers.

One day the creator decided to test the loyalty of the inmates of the garden. He disguised himself as a leper and appeared to them as one suffering from the loathsome disease in its advanced stages. He applied first to the Eyes for assistance, but they drove him away in disgust; he next appeared to the Head and received no better treatment; the Feet and the Hands also refused to succour him. Finally he went to the Stomach who whilst strongly inclined to turn his back on the unsightly object yet remembered the commands of his Creator, and treated the poor beggar kindly before letting him go home.

The next day the Creator sent his messengers to the members he had visited. To the Eyes he sent blindness; to the Head, headaches; and to the Stomach, pain. Áll were commanded to appear at his court. When charged with ungenerous and disloyal conduct, the Stomach was the only one able to plead successfully "not guilty". Hence the Creator decreed that all the other members of the body should for ever be subservient to the Stomach! The Head should carry its food; the Eyes must constantly be watching the way it should take; the Hands were to procure and prepare its food; and the Feet should carry it withersoever it chooses to go!

The Stomach being very stupid, as many young children are (lit), pleaded to be allowed to share the troubles of his brethren. The Creator acceded to his request and therefore appointed that his place should be in the forefront of all - a position which exposed him to many dangers" [2]

The above fable rather tells us something about the origin of man and the cause of the many ailments which plague him. Basden used the word "created" in his translation of this Igbo fable when "made" is the most appropriate word.

This is however a hermeneutical problem. "Creation" understood as "the production of a thing in entirety out of nothingness either of self or subject"[3] is completely alien to the Igbo concept. This is understandably so because the Igbo hold an anthropormorphic view of God.

---

[2] This is one of the many fables collected by Basden. Cf. Basden, G. T., *Among the Ibos of Nigeria*, London, Frank Cass & Co Ltd., 2nd ed. 1966, pp. 282-283.

[3] Gleen, p. J., *Cosmology, a Class Manual in the Philosophy of Bodily Being*, London, B. Herder Book Co. 1949, p. 194.

Here is another rather incredible myth regarding the origin of the world. It was rendered by O. U. Kalu as follows:

"The first man came down by a ladder to find a watery, marshy earth. Somehow, an Awka smith was sent to use his fiery bellow to dry the earth. The problem was now how to feed the new human beings. Their leader, Eru, was asked to kill his eldest son and daughter and plant their heads. From the head of the son sprouted yam and from the head of the daughter sprouted cocoyam. Eru distributed the new products. Even today, yam is the prince of agricultural products and the yam-growing cycle dominate time reckoning and festivals".[4]

In the Igbo cosmogonical concept, there is a chronological order in "creation". *Enu* (the heavens) was the first to be called into existence. In the above mythology, man is seen as coming from the above (*enu*) to find the *Ani* - the earth, in an uninhabitable state. Yam and cocoyam, representing the plant kingdom came into being only after the watery, marshy earth has been dried and made conducive for plant life. There is something of the *Hexahaemeron*[+] in this account of the creation for after all the scriptural word, "yom" which is translated or rather mistranslated as "day" indicates an indefinite period of time.

The following Igbo folklore compiled by Talbot supports the above observation. The folklore itself was narrated by Obi Amara as follows:

"There is a big bird in our bush called *Ogbu-ghu*, known to most Ibo and Kalabari as *Akama-akama* or *Okpoa* (the hornbill). The mother of this bird died. In those days, *Ale* (*Ala, Ana, Ani*) the earth was not; so *Ogbu-ghu* could not find a place to bury his dead. Long time he flew up and down, bearing the body on his back. Then he thought: 'My old mother! No Place to bury her'. Therefore he made her a grave upon his head. That is why this bird has a mound upon his head to this day".

"After a while, as *Ogbu-ghu* flew over the water seeking a resting-place, but finding none, he saw one fine woman and one man, both big too much, swimming in the water. He watched and saw that they were making something. Not much long after land began to appear. When this had grown quite a big land, Ali cried: "When any man dies, let him be buried here". Her own body she stretched over the land. She it is who made all, both the

---

4 *Cf. Readings In African Humanities African Cultural Development*, ed.. by Kalu O. U., University of Nigeria Nsukka, Enugu, Fourth Dimension Pub. Co. Ltd., p. 38.

+ Six days of creation.

earth itself and the crops. When the dead are buried they turn to earth. That is why our people say: "We are of the same skin with Ali".

"Trees too she brought; *Oji* tree (the Iroko, *Chlorophora excelsa*) was the first. The second was *Akpu* (the silk cotton tree, *Bombax giganteus* and third *Odala* (*Khaya Mahogany*). It is to this one that a woman prays and sacrifices when she wants piccan. Next, Ali brought the kola tree, also named Oji, the fruit of which is set out for ghost offering...".[5]

Just before we conclude this section, it is relevant to examine the cosmogonical ideas of a prominent Igbo elder from Ihembosi as it is expressed in his dialogue with R. C. Arazu. Arazu initiated the dialogue with a series of questions among which are the following:

Question: "This *Chukwu*
We call on *Chukwu*
We call on Sun-and-king-of-upper-regions
(*Anyanwu-na-Eze-Enu*)
Another man say:
Olisa - ebili-uwa (*Osebuluwa*)
What is the difference between them?

Answer: The difference between them is this,
That we came into being,
And saw that this thing, here,
Is called 'the goat',
And that is called 'the fowl',
And this called 'the man';
And in that way everything on earth,
Everything that has the power to move,
Or even the tree that is on the ground,
They are as we saw them.
It is said that *Chukwu* brought them,
That *Chukwu* placed them here,
That He left them.
It is *Chukwu* and this Earth (*Ana*)
On which we stand
They, we are told,
Own all men
Who put the hand into the mouth
And all the trees,

---

[5] Talbot, P. A., *Tribes of the Niger Delta*, London, the sheldom Press, 1932, p. 26.

And each and everything;
It is the same *Chukwu*
And this *Ana* (Earth)
Who brought out man and put him up;
We are not witnesses;
We are saying
What we were told".[6]

The Ihembosi elder's concept may have been somehow adulterated by some western notions. Nevertheless, the concept of the world as made by God and *Ana*, which is recurrent motif in Igbo cosmogony is once more emphasized. Emerging from the above fables, myth and dialogue are the following facts about Igbo Cosmology:

I.   That the origin of the world is traceable to a wonderful Being, Chukwu (God);
II.   That the action of God is needed always to uphold the cosmic structure and order. (*Chukwu Seraka, Uwa agwu*" - If God withholds his Hands instantly the world must end");
III. That there is some chronological order in creation.

Cosmic Dynamism: An Igbo Tenet

The term dynamism is taken from the Greek word '*dynamis*' which means 'force' or 'power'. Thus dynamism by reason of its etymology suggests some theory of power or force as the explanation for the material world.

Force is a living concept of the African world. According to Temples:

> The Africans speak, act and live, as if for them beings were forces.... Force, for them is the nature of being, force is being, being is force.[7]

While the west may speak of gradation of beings, Africans speak of the gradations of forces. This same concept pervades Igbo thought-pattern. Since being is force and everything is a kind of force, it follows that existence is dynamic including of course the material world.

Though the concept of separate beings, of substances, to use scholastic terminology is alien to Igbo thought, there is something of *hylomorphism* in their concept about the constitution of the world. *Chi* is the substantial form that gives matter its identity. Njaka puts it as follows:

---

[6] This is part of the dialogue between Arazu and Ezenwadeyi, an elder of Ihembosi as reproduced by Elizabeth Isichei, Cf. Isichei, E., *Igbo Worlds*, London, Macmillan Educational Limited, 1977, p. 171-172.

[7] Temples, P., *Bantu Philosophy*, Paris, Presence Africaine, 1969, pp. 51-52.

The *Chi* may be compared to the substantial form in matter. The *Chi* is the essence of any existence, animate or inanimate....[8]

The *Chi*, besides being a substantial form in matter is also the active force that give individuality to every individual. One is that which his *chi* makes him.

Cosmic dynamism or the theory of force as the explanation of the material world, a view strongly held by the Igbo, has considerable impact on Igbo social and religious activities. We shall see the extent of this impact in the next section.

Igbo Metaphysical World

For the Igbo, there exist two worlds - the world of man and the spirit world. One is as real as the other. The Igbo world of man or the material real world has been discussed under cosmology which is a philosophical science of material real being. Metaphysics, (with its subject matters as God, Freedom and Immortality according to Immanuel Kant) is concerned rather with non-material real being. The Igbo concept of God and immortality will be more appropriately treated under metaphysics. Because of the importance of getting a handle on these Igbo notions, and because of the confused way in which they are frequently conceived, I am obliged to adopt this division for the sake of clarity.

In the world of spirits, *Chukwu* ranks the highest. *Chukwu* is the great First Cause. He is the maker of both gods and men. He is bounteous and benevolent yet He is regarded as being too far away from man's comprehension. *Chi-ukwu* - great *Chi* (to distinguish Him from the personal *Chi* of whom we shall speak later) is regarded as being too remote from man to need either shrine or worship. Petitions to *Chukwu* must pass through some "medium" or "messengers" before it reaches him.

The Igbo sense of reverence and awe towards God, is evident in some of the descriptive names used to qualify God. Besides *Chi-ukwu* - "the Supreme Being", He is called *Chi-ne-ke* - "the Being that creates". His other names include: *Osebuluwa* - the Being that carries the world"; *Obasi* - "the Being that is ubiquitous"; *Olisa* - "the sustaining penetrating Being"; *Eze-Elu* - "King of the heavens"; *Eze Igwe* - "King of the Sky"; and many others.

The Igbo hold an anthropomorphic view of God. God's residence is thought by the traditional Igbo to be located somewhere in the skies. Hence the name *Eze-Igwe* - "King of the sky. Of course, since *Chukwu* oversees

---

[8] Njaka, E. N., *op. cit.* p. 32.

the world and supervises the activities of the minor deities, he must occupy a place above the earth. Talbot recorded the following from the Igbo among whom he lived:

> Chi is our chief God. We regard her as of feminine gender, because everything was created by her. For the same reason *Ali*, the Earth Mother is looked upon as a woman, since she bears our crops and that which gives birth cannot be other than the feminine.[9]

Of course, that God should be so conceived in a feminine gender is no surprise for as I had pointed out earlier on, the notion of creation *ex nihilo* is entirely alien to Igbo thought. Since it is the nature of female things to produce or reproduce, to bring forth things, then *Chi-ukwu* from whom all things ultimately come must have this nature.

We have noted that *Chukwu* - the Supreme Being is the highest of all metaphysical beings. He is far removed from the ordinary affairs of men. Yet he manifests Himself in all created things. This manifestation of God in all created things is called *Chi*. This concept is very vital in Igbo traditional thought and life as we shall explain shortly.

Chi - Igbo Ontology

Chi is God's manifestation in all created things. It is held by the Igbo that *Chi* is that divine force directly involved with the affairs of men. Everyone has his own *Chi*. It is the personal *Chi* who arranges the life of every individual. Whenever she thinks it good to take a man away, that man dies. *Chi* fixes the destiny of everyone right from birth.

A *Chi* is spiritual substance and therefore immortal. In fact, it is the life-giving and sustaining essence of a living man. The *Chi* leaves a man at death and its exit from man is what is called death because the *Chi* is likened to the breath of life. The *Chi* being a divine force is thought to be omniscient, can foresee danger, and is concerned only with the individual with whom it remains throughout his life time. Njaka noted as follows:

> The *Chi* may be compared to the substantial form in matter. The *Chi* is the essence of any existence, animate or inanimate, but in man it is highest and has the most intelligence. The higher an object the higher its *Chi*. The *Chi* sustains all beings and forms all things. It can be likened to the creative intelligence of God.[10]

---

9 Talbot, P. A., *op. cit.* p. 19.
10 Njaka, E. N., *op. cit.* p. 32.

Every adult male is expected to erect a shrine for his *Chi* as soon as he builds a house of his own. So also is every Igbo woman expected to do when she takes a husband. The shrine is usually sited infront of the house. The husband and the wife may have shrines adjacent to each other's. In the event of continuous ill-luck or other misfortunes, the way out is to placate one's Chi by a ritual offering.

The role of *Chi* in an individual's life evokes a kind of fatalism. Surely, if the Igbo believe that one's fate is entirely in the hands of *Chi* and is determined by him, then relying on this belief, he would very readily accept life's happenings with blind resignation which tantamounts to fatalism. Obviously, there is some element of fatalism in this but the Igbo is careful not to let his fatalism relapse into mere quietism. For though the Igbo believes that his fate is determined by his *Chi*, he nevertheless hopes that a bad fate can be changed either by placating his *Chi* or by other forms of negotiations with other spiritual forces. Infact, for the Igbo, manipulation and negotiation are a way of getting on in life, because for him, life is like a market.

One curious thing about the *Chi* is its individuality and universality. Its individuality lies in the fact that every creature has its own personal *Chi*. No two individuals have the same *Chi*. An Igbo saying has it that, "*Otu nne muru, ma obughi otu Chi kere*." Rendered literally, it means, "born of one mother but not created by one *Chi*". This saying is often quoted to explain why in a family constellation, different shades of character and temperaments are identifiable. It also explains why members of the same nuclear family do not have equal fortune. Thus the *Chi* expresses itself differently in different individuals. It has been pointed out that although the *Chi* plays a determining role in one's life; in his success or failure, it does not usually force the individual to blind compliance. There is room for co-operation. Thus, the Igbo say, "*Onye kwe, chi ya ekwe*" - "If one says, yes, his *Chi* will say the same". This is to say that the *Chi* is always at the side of any individual determined to succeed.

The universality of *Chi*, on the other hand lies in the fact that *Chi*, as the manifestation of the Great *Chi* - *Chi-ukwu*, and as the essence of any existence, animate and inanimate, is in all things. It is the universal "breath" of the Great *Chi*, God, received by every creature in accordance with its capacity and nature.

There arises from the Igbo concept of *Chi* this one theological fact - that everybody possesses some godhead, some divinity. This is a simple syllogism resulting from the premises that the *Chi* is the divine force, the active manifestation of God in his creature and that every human being has his own *Chi* and not only human beings but all creatures at large. This is why the Igbo natural religion is popularly described as animism.

Apart from *Chi-ukwu* and *Chi*, there are other kindred beings in the metaphysical world believed by the Igbo to exercise considerable influence in the material world. For the Igbo society happens to be a place where men live in a covenant with spirits as well as in a covenant with *Chukwu* and man. Men and spirits commingle and communicate with each other on an everyday basis. The next to be considered among these spirits is the ancestral spirits.

Ancestral Spirits

To begin with, there are two categories of spirits - those created as such, and those which were once human beings. The ancestors are the departed of up to five generations whose memories still linger within their families. These are said to be in personal immortality. The ancestors are only physically dead but otherwise they are still alive. Mbiti prefers the term "living-dead" in qualifying this category of spirit to the other terms "ancestral spirits" or "ancestors". He argues that ancestral spirits or ancestors are misleading terms since they imply only those spirits who were once the ancestors of the living. To avoid an obvious ambiguity that arises from the term "living-dead", I shall maintain the use of ancestral spirits or ancestors.

Now, the ancestors are as it were a bridge that ensure a smooth flow of transcendental traffic between the physical and the metaphysical worlds. It is an accredited belief in Igboland that the ancestors are only partly dead and partly alive. They are part and parcel of their human families and people have personal memories of them. The ancestors are still people known by their personal names and have not yet become "things" or impersonal spirits. A "good" burial is a passport to the spirit world - the happy dwelling place of the ancestors.

The Igbo have a reverential regard for the ancestors. Of all other spirits, the ancestors are the closest to the human families. They return to their respective families from time to time, and share meal with them, however, symbolically. In a typical Igbo family, before the meal, the head of the family usually takes some lumps of food, dip it into the soup and throw it outside for the ancestors who are believed to be hovering around though invisible to ordinary men. By so doing the Igbo demonstrates his belief in the ever-presence of the ancestors.

The ancestors know and do have interest in what is going on in their family. When they appear usually to the oldest member of the household, they are recognised by name as "so and so"; they inquire about the family affairs, and may even warn of any impending danger or rebuke those who have failed to follow their special instructions.

The ancestors are best group of intermediaries between men and God because they are mid-way between the spirit-world and human world. It is this belief in the personal immortality; in the spiritual presence of the ancestors that gave rise to the "cult of ancestors". If you ask the Igbo man why he "worships" the ancestors he will reply: "They are in the happy land of the spirits, in the headquarters, and will not forget their children". As spirits, the ancestors have power to protect their beloved ones in the human world against evil spirits and evil men; against misfortune and other calamities. Being part and parcel of their respective *umunna* (family), they endeavour to safeguard their families from being populated by "*Akaliogoli*" or "*Ndiberibe*" - people who are worthless and without foundation.

The spiritual presence and company of the ancestors are cherished by the Igbo. However, frequent appearance of the ancestors is not regarded as a blessing. When an ancestor appears very frequently to members of his family, a fortune-teller is consulted to ascertain the cause of the frequent appearances. When the cause has been thus ascertained due care is taken to perform the prescribed rites to pacify the restless ancestral spirit.

It is the Igbo traditional belief that an ancestor can simultaneously retain his place as an ancestor; be the incarnation of the ancestor in one or more living persons, and hope to be re-incarnated in one or more persons yet unborn. In other words, the ancestor potentially occupies "Three worlds" - the worlds of the dead, of the living and of the unborn and influences all of them by means of "*iluo uwa*". This unique position of an ancestor makes him very important in the social, political and religious life of the Igbo - a position aspired by every traditional Igbo.

An offense against the ancestors is an outright abomination and thus a crime against *Ala*, the constitutional deity. No Igbo wants to become a wandering spirit at death through having lost favour with the ancestors and thus denied a welcome into the *Ala-Muo* - the spirit world, by one's ancestors and also denied subsequent reincarnation. An Igbo, therefore must always be in harmony with his family - *umunna* so that he will get a good burial which is a passport to the *Ala-muo*. This same consideration induces him to active participation in political and social affairs of his polity because he must maintain a proud and worthy record on earth if he is to attain honourable acceptance in *Ala-muo*. The more a person accomplishes on earth, the higher his status in *Ala-muo*, from where he hopes to be reincarnated as an outstanding man or woman.[11]

Thus, the cult of ancestors engenders social harmony and moral rectitude and fosters communal spirit. It urges the Igbo on to great achievements and to strive for high status in the society. Above all, the "ancestral cult" mellows the natural fear arising from man's uncertainty of his fate after his earthly sojourn. And what is more, it enhances inter-communication and interaction between the physical and the metaphysical worlds.

Other Spirits

Other important spirits worthy of mention include "*Mbataku*" - the spirit of wealth, and "*Agwu*". *Mbataku* is imagined to be a ram-headed spirit to whom the Igbo attribute their wealth. It is a common practice in Igboland to make a sacrifice to *Mbataku* before setting out for a journey. Only a piece of kola can serve this purpose. In the event of the journey being successful, *Mbataku* to whom the success is imputed is rewarded accordingly. When trading faces a slump, *Mbataku* is requested to provide better economic opportunities. If an animal strays into the compound and all efforts to locate the owner fail, the animal is killed on the *Mbataku* shrine, the spirit of wealth, claiming the blood, while men feast on the carcass. *Mbataku* is a friendly spirit and the Igbo are well disposed towards it unlike "*agwu isi*" - head spirit which is held in horror. Perhaps the only Igbo willing to discuss "*agwu*" are its servitors who talk of their early encounter with "*agwu*", their long struggle to avoid it and how they finally agreed to serve it.

Agwu is the most proselytizing spirit always is need of servitors. It is envious of people's wealth, which paradoxically, it claims to bring. To serve "*agwu*" is to enter the long rites of ordination which may eventually make one a *dibia* (medicine man). Not many people have the wealth and patience to attain this height. Some stop after the initial rites or at any stage of the ordination process where they feel they can confidently challenge *agwu* to provide the economic resources necessary to complete the rites. But to refuse *agwu's* call to its service is to face a long trial and temptation, involving loss of property, loss of children, barrenness, and, in many cases "*ara or ala agwu*" - psychosomatic syndromes. The effective weapon with which to combat "*ara agwu*" is the performance of "*ilu-agwu*", a not very pleasant rite.

---

11 Reincarnation is called "iluo uwa - "a return to the world".

Mention must be made of *aha njoku* or *ife joku*, the yam spirit. *Ife-joku* is a powerful spirit respected by the Igbo. Because this powerful spirit is associated with yam, the crop has acquired some social and religious importance. Within each agricultural cycle every farmer offers about three sacrifices to *Ife-jioku*: at the beginning of the farming season; the first harvest and the final harvest. Devout priests and villagers do not eat "new" yam until a formal sacrifice is made to *Ife-jioku*. *Ife-jioku* is not a harmful spirit. However, people may incur its displeasure by any form of abuse of yam seeds. Quarreling on the yam farm is an offence and egg is usually broken on the spot to ask for the forgiveness of *Ife-jioku*.

It has to be noted that *Ala* - the Earth goddess, *Anyanwu* - the sun-god are not spirits as such. They are simply thought by the Igbo to possess some "supernatural principle". Thus they do not qualify as metaphysical realities. This also is the position of *Alusi* which is a physical object with a spiritual significance.

These may be better discussed under Igbo religious creeds rather than under metaphysics.

Immortality

It has already been noted that man is thought by the Igbo to be a composite of spiritual and material substances. The *Chi* is that spiritual life-giving and life-sustaining principle which animates the body - the material substance. In this sense, this is the "soul" of the body. In the other sense, the soul called *mkpulu-Obi* in Igbo is not the same as *Chi*. The soul is the vital principle whose departure from the body is what we call death. The time of its departure is estimated to be the moment the last breath is drawn or when earth is put on the corpse in the grave. The soul may still hang round the grave for some time to receive gifts and consultation. For the Igbo, the soul never dies. This is partly proved by their belief in reincarnation at least in the case of children, and partly by the "cult" of the ancestors about which we have spoken.[12]

One practical demonstration of the Igbo belief in immortality is the practice of masquerading, the *muo* or *mmanwu* or *egwugwu* society. In the words of C. K. Meek;

> *muo* are infact ancestral spirits personated by maskers who appear in public at seasonal periods, at festival and at celebrations of final funeral rites. [13]

---

[12] Cf. see the section on ancestral spirit.

[13] Meek, C., *Law and Authority in a Nigerian Tribe*, London, 1937, p. 15.

Thus the *muo* or *mmanwu* are believed to be the dead come to life for special celebrations. They speak in a strange, guttural voices and are believed to emerge from the underworld through a tiny hole in the ground. The "*mmuo*" are saluted as "our father"! "owner of the village"! etc.

At this juncture, it is necessary to point out the obvious link between the concept of immortality and the institution of marriage. So long as there are persons in the family who remember someone who is physically dead, that person is not really dead; he is still alive in the minds of his relatives and neigbours who knew him while he was in human form. His name still remains something personal, and he can "appear" to members of his family who would recognise him by name. It is in one's own family that the "dead" is kept in personal memory for the longest time after their physical death.

It is no wonder therefore why it is a big concern to elderly men in Igboland if a young man waited too long before getting married. Such young men are sternly warned: "if you do not marry and get children, when you die you will be thrown away as a waste matter, no one will remember you again". A person who has no descendants in effect quenches the fire of life, and becomes fore-ever dead since his line of physical continuation is blocked if he does not get married and bear children.

The stage of personal immortality which last as long as there are people who still keep personal memory of the deceased, is externalised by the physical continuation of the traits of their parents or progenitors. Procreation is the absolute way of insuring that a person is not cut off from personal immortality. Unfortunate therefore is the man or woman who has nobody to "remember" him after his physical death. To lack someone close to him who will ensure his personal immortality is the worst misfortune that may befall any Igbo man. To die without getting married and without children is to be completely cut off from the human society; to be disconnected, to be an outcast and to lose all links with mankind.

When the deceased has passed the stage of personal immortality and has now moved on to the stage of full spirits, and admitted into the company of spirits, people then lose contact and personal interest in them. Certainly at this stage, their names must have been forgotten and their memory out of mind. But such deceased persons pass into the class of the unnamed ancestors of the clan. This may be said to be the stage of collective immortality.

It has to be noted that the Igbo believe that one's social position is to be maintained after death, in the "hereafter". This explains why an *"Ozo"* titled man is usually buried with special rites. Indeed, burial ceremony of titled men is very expensive and very tedious. Funerals in general are the last transitional rites, introducing a man into the world of the spirits.

Reincarnation

The Igbo's belief in reincarnation is closely linked with their belief in immortality. It is strongly held by the Igbo that an ancestor could be reborn in a child. The particular ancestor so reborn is recognised in the child. When there is doubt as to which ancestor has reincarnated, the fortune-teller may be consulted. The child believed to be a reincarnated ancestor is addressed sometimes by the name of the ancestor. If the child, for instance is a male, members of the family, especially the aged ones usually address him as "*nna ayi*", or "*nna*" - "our father" or "father". Such a child is given due respect as befitting the ancestor who has reincarnated in him or her.

Not only are people born again of the same or another mother but also children who die young are believed to have decided before hand in their group when they would die, especially if they did not like their family. These children are called "*Ogbanje*" - "Repeaters". This writer has met a number of Igbo men and women who claim to be "*Ogbanje*".

The belief in reincarnation and the "cult of ancestors" seem to contradict each other. But this apparent contradiction is resolved when we remember that only part of the ancestor's spirit is believed born again. Father Temples says that this is explicable by the philosophy of force. The ancestor does not create the child. Africans do not hold that for they know that God does this. It is not strictly the ancestral spirit that is reborn, but the child is supposed to come under his particular influence and to have received part of his vitality and qualities. If this explanation is noted, then the apparent illogicality is eliminated.

The Hereafter

For the majority of African people, the hereafter is only a continuation of life more or less as it is in its human form. This means that personalities are retained, social and political status are maintained, sex distinction is continued, human activities are reproduced in the hereafter; the wealth and poverty of the individuals remain unchanged, and in many ways the hereafter is a carbon copy of the present life.

The Igbo locate the Hereafter in the under-world. This is probably the logical interment of the body in the ground. The hereafter is inhabited by only the spirits. However, the belief in the ever-presence of the ancestors in the human families coupled with the conviction that the ancestors play an important role in their family suggest that the hereafter is the "geographical here".

Igbo Natural Religion

The phrase Igbo *Natural Religion* is used here to clearly distinguish it from *supernatural* or *revealed* religion like christianity which is just a little above one hundred years old in Igboland. Religion in general involves a supreme Being and man on one hand and God-man relationship on the other hand. Man expressed this relationship in forms of worship, sacrifice, rituals etc which he regards as his obligation towards God. Thus the Scholastics define religion as "a complex of truth and duties by which man's relationship with God is established and expressed". Now, Natural Religion would consist of a complex of truth and duties which man discovers by his own reason. So, whereas many authors preferred to talk of Igbo *traditional* religion, I would rather speak of Igbo *natural* religion. The latter phrase aptly describes the form of religion practised and is still practised in Igboland before the advent of Christianity.

Originally, the Igbo natural religion was not known by any particular name for it was not founded by anyone; it sprouted from the land as it were, and grew up naturally watered by the spring of religious sentiments of the Igbo people.

In recent time however, the Igbo natural religion has been disparaginly termed paganism by the early pious missionaries to whom the religion was unintelligible. Currently, the term animism is widely used to describe the religion. Neither of these terms are acceptable to Igbo scholars. These terms are at the best a misnomer for they relate to the superficial and not to the essentials of the Igbo religion. All things considered, "*Ofoism*" is a more realistic and more practical name for the Igbo natural religion. It is coined from the word *Ofo* which is the most significant symbol in the Igbo natural religion, and the prefix "ism". *Ofoism* was first used by Njaka to designate the Igbo religion.[14]

Ojike Mbonu calls the religion "*Omenana*", which literally means "happening in the land" but otherwise means, "custom" and may also be interpreted as "constitution". We are here[15] not mainly concerned with the problem of terminology. In what follows, *Ofoism* should be understood as synonymous with Igbo natural religion.

Ofoism is a religion with one major mission namely to establish a harmonious relationship between man, "*Chukwu*" and other spirits. It is

---

[14] Njaka, E. N., *Igbo Political Culture*, Evanton, Northwestern University Press, 1974, p. 28.
[15] Mbonu, O., *op. cit.*, pp. 15-155.

basically a non-aggressive and non-proselytising religion. *Ọfọism* operates on the platform of religious democracy. It is a sensitive religion that caters for the spiritual, moral and social dimensions of man. *Ọfọism* is not an "opium"' of the people. The belief that a man's social status and achievement here in this life would be transferred to the "hereafter" encourages the adherents to strive hard to attain high and respectable goals in this life. Hence, *Ọfọism* is a progressive religion.

What needs to be considered now is the creed of *Ọfọism*. But since these have been extensively discussed under the Igbo metaphysical world, it would be unnecessary to repeat them here. But we can summarise the beliefs as follows:

1. Belief in Chukwu, the Supreme Being - God
2. Belief in other minor deities (nature gods)
3. Belief in other spirits (good and evil ones)
4.' Belief in reincarnation
5. Belief in immortality
6. Belief in reward and punishment for good or evil done on earth.

Let us now have a look at some important symbols, places and personalities in the Igbo natural religion.

Ọfọ

Ọfọ is the most important symbol in the Igbo religion. Its religious value lies not in its material form but in its symbolic representation. Materially, it is a piece of wood from about four to more than twelve inches long, carved from the wood of *Detarium elastica*, or *Detarium senegalensis*. A typical *Ọfọ* resembles a club. The material nature of the *Ọfọ* is not important. Its importance lies in its symbolism.

> *Ọfọ* is the central symbol of the Igbo religion. In addition to being a staff of authority, it is an emblem symbolising the links between *Chukwu* and man, the dead and the living, the living and the unborn. The *Ọfọ* also symbolises justice, righteousness, and truth.[16]

The *Ọfọ* has a central position in all major religious, social and even political activities. For instance, titles are conferred with the *Ọfọ*. Laws are ratified and consecrated with the *Ọfọ* and none is valid without it being used.

An Igbo male is not regarded as independent or mature until he acquires his own personal *Ọfọ*. Usually, after he has reached puberty and has

---

[16] Njaka, E. N., *op. cit.*, p. 35.

undergone an initiation ceremony, he is regarded as an adult and only then may he proceed to take his personal *Ọfọ* in another ceremony. Acquiring the *Ọfọ* raises him to a new social and religious status and confers on him the authority to communicate with *Chukwu* and his ancestors from whom the unborn come. Hence with the *Ọfọ*, the individualisation of the Igbo adult male is functionally established.

All *Ọfọ* are not of equal importance and status. The *Ọfọ* are classed under two main categories namely, the ancestral *Ọfọ* and the individual *Ọfọ* acquired at maturity by males. The ancestral *Ọfọ* is handed down from generation to generation. As long as an *Ọfọ* continues to pass from generation to generation, it is believed that the person who first handed it down is by the fact of the *Ọfọ* 's continued existence also alive.

Like the individual, each social or political unit has its own *Ọfọ* which is separate from and greater than any individual's *Ọfọ* in that unit. Furthermore, the unit head's personal *Ọfọ* takes precedence over any other *Ọfọ* in that polity. The village *Ọfọ* is greater than the family *Ọfọ* and that of the village-group is greater than the village *Ọfọ*. Usually, the *Okpara* is the holder of the family *Ọfọ* Because of this he performs a leading role is all political and religious functions. A devout *Ọfọ* holder says his daily prayers fervently with his *Ọfọ* placed on the ground, He stands as the intermediary between the living lineage members and the dead ancestors. He offers sacrifices, presides over swearing rites and is expected to participate in the legislative, executive and the judicial activities of the village.

The *Ọfọ* is possessed exclusively by the adult males. Their female counterparts used the "*umune*" in the same way as an *Ọfọ* is used by the adult males with this one difference that the *umune* cannot be carried about like the *Ọfọ*. No special initiation ceremony is required for the right to its use. Its physical representation is a small tree known by the same name as the leaf, which leaf is used whenever the *umune* is deemed necessary. It is evident from what has been said above that the *Ọfọ* is the cornerstone of the Igbo natural religion.

Ogu

The *ogu* is more of a religious concept than a physical object. The *ogu* stands for innocence. As a concept, it can be symbolised by anything be it a stick or a stone, during an appropriate ceremony. They *ogu* can be invoked on the following occasions:

i.   When a person is enumerating the injuries done to him by another person while declaring his own innocence;

ii.   When taking an oath, the individual uses sticks to enumerate the specific issues involved in the oath on which he declares his innocence;

iii. During an *"Igbandu"* ceremony. *"Igbandu"* is a formal oath for re-establishing confidence, in which one may drink the blood of the other.

The *Ogu* concept is still alive today in Igboland.

Igbo Oracles

The Oracles are sacred chambers where men go to consult the spirits. In direct communication with the invisible spirit, the pilgrim may inquire from the unseen concerning a bewildering unknown. The most prominent of Igbo oracles are the *Agbala* of Awka, the *Igwe* of Umunoha, the *Kamalu* of Ozuzu and the *Ibini okpabe* of Arochukwu also known as the "long juju" of Arochukwu.

The Igbo believe in the veracity of oracular verdicts and "revelations" because of the spell of mystery that surrounds them and also for the fact that many who have consulted them appeared to have realised their objectives. The ability of each oracle to attract clients depends largely on its credibility which is usually established after its predictions or verdicts have been put to test and found reliable on several occasions. This is why the "long juju" of Arochukwu attained a position of supremacy over the others and was recognised as the most influential Igbo oracle.

Each oracle is entrusted to the care of a powerful priest. The cost of consulting an oracle is prohibitive and people choose that line of action when other means of resolving an issue of delicate and often dangerous nature have failed to yield the desired result. Or where a deceased relative must be consulted for one reason or the other.

Viewed from a critical point, the oracles are run by a network of "intelligent" officials who are well versed in local and "foreign" affairs. Since no client as a rule goes directly to the oracle except through a chain of contact agents, it was possible to ascertain through the relays of these agents what the clients' problem was.

Whatever the limitations of the oracular practice may be, it nevertheless plays a vital religious role for besides their judicial role as the final court of appeal in Igboland, the oracular verdict or predictions normally ratify popular opinions and prejudices. Above all, by having recourse to the oracles, the burden of making a difficult but necessary decision is thus transferred from the human to the spiritual or rather supernatural domain.

Dibia (The Native Priests)

The word "*Dibia*" is loosely and widely used in Igbo country to describe various functionaries. A diviner, a herbalist or a medicine man may be called a *Dibia*. But in the strict sense of the word, which is what is adopted in this discourse, a *dibia* is one who has performed *igwo aja* - the rite of ordination. A *dibia* is only authorised to perform all priestly functions after this ordination ceremony. He is not however obliged to exercise his priestly functions. At the ordination, the priest is infused with the power to "see" things", the power of vision (*ihu ohu*). Being able to "see things", - he can divine though most *dibia* do not exercise this power of vision. Membership of the *dibia* "fraternity" is strictly by ordination. Seniority in the *dibia* congregation is based on the order of initiation and not on age.

The *dibia* are generally respected and they enjoy certain immunities. Even in the "dark" age of Igbo history when long travel outside one's community was fraught with serious danger, only the dibia could without fear of being harmed or molested undertake distant journeys.

As we have noted, religion plays such a central and unifying role in Igbo life that it permeates all the crevices of the Igbo society. Certainly, neither the culture nor the political or legal systems of the Igbo can be understood without due reference to their religion.

Igbo Native Morality

Igbo religion and morality are closely interwoven. In fact they are not only complementary but also inseparable. In spite of this marriage of morality and religion there is nevertheless a well defined code of morality in Igbo society. G.T. Basden testifies that:

> In the majority of Ibo towns a very clearly defined codes of morals exist theoretically. Infringements on these laws may lead to severe penalties being inflicted....[17]

Chukwu, the Supreme Being, is not regarded by the Igbo as the arbiter in moral issues. The earth-goddess, *Ani* and the ancestors are believed to punish every breach of morality especially the very grave ones.

Igbo moral ethics revolve around justice. The just man in the Igbo moral estimation is one who gives to every one what is his due; one who tells the truth regardless of who or what is at stake; one who is objective in his judgment. For the Igbo the classical sinner is the thief. This is because theft is seen as an aggression and an infringement on other people's rights which is a violation of social justice.

---

[17] Basden, G.T., *op. cit.*, p. 34.

Thus, so dreadful and so grave is the act of theft that a thief is denied even by his own kith and kin. It is normally said, "*Onye ori aburo nwanne madu*". A thief is nobody's brother). It is this same sense of justice which drives the Igboman to justify revenge and to say, "*eme mbolu abughi ajo ihe*" (to revenge of wrong done is not wrong). Praying that justice be done, the Igbo prays: "*Egbe belu ugo belu nke si ibe ya ebena nku kapu ya*! (let the kite perch and let the eagle perch, whichever says that the other will not perch let its wings break off!).

So much has to be said of Igbo religion and morality here. It will be seen from what follows that religion is an indispensable instrument in achieving social harmony; sound political order, and the maintenance of high moral standards in Igbo society. In the words of Njaka:

> *Ofoism*, therefore, is highly social and political; it has been successfully used to sanctify laws and this prevent their violation. The Igbo has utilized his religion in the regulation of social order, in the adjudication of cases, and in the maintenance of effective administration.[18]

This fact about the Igbo natural religion must be borne in mind throughout our discussion.

Chapter 3

The Nature Of Igbo Laws

Laws in the traditional Igbo society are not codified. Though unwritten, they are nevertheless quite comprehensible. In practice, the Igbo are aware that the laws that regulate their lives are not of the same nature. They are obviously conscious of the fact that all laws are not of equal importance. Implicit therefore in the Igbo concept of law is the fact that laws are of various categories. But the native Igbo is more concerned with the practical divisions of laws rather than their theoretical segmentation. Undoubtedly, the Igbo traditional laws would be better understood and appreciated if these practical divisions of law have corresponding theoretical opposite numbers. This is the task of an Igbo philosopher and this is what I venture to do.

Divine Laws

The first category of laws that are easily discernible in the multifarious spectrum of Igbo body of laws are the divine laws. Divine here means pertaining to God, originating from God, tending towards God. M.M. Green, a British anthropologist, has this to say on this legal aspect of Igbo life:

> Legal rules are of two main classes and are recognised as such. There are those which might be called ordinary human laws and those whose breach is held to be not only illegal but also an offence against a supernatural power and particularly against *Ala*, the land. Of the perpetrator of such an offence it would be said: *"Omeruru ala"* - "he polluted the land". Such offences are usually distinguished from merely natural offences.[1]

The latter of the two classes I have classified as divine laws. For the breach of these laws is regarded as offence not only against human society alone but directly against the supernatural. The characteristic features of these divine laws are:

---

[1] Green, M.M., *Ibo Village Affairs*, New York, Frederick A. Praeger, 1964, p. 100.

1. They were not made by man.
2. Their violation carry heavy penalties.
3. In addition to the punishment, a propitiatory rite or sacrifice must be performed.
4. A supernatural wrath is believed to have been provoked which sometimes may sweep across the entire community.

Let us examine each of these features individually. Some of the offences which are regarded as "*nso*" or "*alu*", which is a breach of the divine laws include incest (defined as sexual intercourse with a person one cannot marry for reason of their blood relationship), homicide, patricide and killing of sacred animals to mention but a few.

Historically, these laws were not known to have passed through any of the legislative processes already described in the preceding chapters in order to become laws. They seem to have been written in the hearts of the Igbo *ab ovo*. If you ask the Igbo about the origin of these laws, he would simply answer: "They are our *omenala* that is to say our custom. And *omenala* is as old as the origin of man himself. This apparent inability to trace these laws to any historical source or to any source whatsoever brings to the fore the other side of the divine law as the natural law. This will be examined in more detail later in this chapter.

The breach of the divine laws carries heavy penalties. Offenders are automatically interdicted from the society until the stain of their crime has been wiped away from the land usually only after the appropriate propitiatory rituals have been performed. The conception is that one who is out of favour with *Ani* - the earth deity is not worthy to live among the community of men, whose parent is the goddess, *Ani*. Thus, incest, whether it was mother-son incest or sister-brother incest, is punishable by a sale of the persons concerned into slavery or similar penalty.

Homicide is even more grave. If a villager kills another man, the murderer is expected to hang himself. There is no provision for the public or private execution of murderer in Igboland. To shed another person's blood under any circumstance is an abomination. This is why the murderer must hang himself. The villagers may however exert serious psychological and social pressure on the murderer but cannot go beyond that.

If the murderer has fled, his family must also flee, and their property is confiscated. Whenever the murderer is caught, he will be made to hang himself to enable the *umu okpu* (daughters of the lands) to perform their cleansing rites. Thus, the necessity of the murderer hanging himself as far as the villagers are concerned, lies in the fact that without the death of the murderer, the *umu okpu* can not perform the rites of *izafu ntu ochu* (sweeping away the ashes of murder). Failure to perform this rites has grave consequences which are dreaded by the villagers.

An offence against *Ala*, that is a breach of the divine law, could bring disaster on the whole village. When there is a frequent occurrence of death of villagers, when there is a sweeping epidemics and other such calamities, it is a sign that something has gone wrong somewhere. In such circumstances, an elderly woman would take money and go to the *dibia* to ascertain the cause of the calamities. The *dibia* would first ask whether anyone has offended *Ala*, in other words, whether any member of the community has broken the divine laws. If this is not known, he would declare that the earth deity is angry for some abomination committed by someone in the community. He would then recommend that ritual sacrifice be immediately offered to placate the goddess.

What should strike us here is the fundamentality of these divine laws. The divine laws are there to protect the lives of the individuals in the community, to safeguard the basic moral principles of the people and to guide the society in its effort to maintain its link with the spiritual community of the spirit world.

The above observations become evident when one recalls the fact that the Igbo natural religion, *Ofoism*, permeates every aspect of their life and tend to engulf their field of law. Njaka noted that:

> Laws and order are maintained because the ancestors so desire and *oha* so command. And the ancestors so desire law and order because *Chukwu* must have approved them.[2]

The divine nature of those laws the breach of which are regarded as abomination - *nso* is further demonstrated by the fact that only a supernatural tribune could dispense justice in case of their breach. For instance, it is not usual for the Igbo to put a man suspected of homicide on trial. The Igbo believe that any case involving a human life is no longer within human jurisdiction. Thus, if a villager assaults another villager and kills him, then there is a clear evidence that murder has been committed. Such a villager is required to hang himself and the villagers will bring pressure to bear on him to do so. But the situation is different when there is no material evidence to prove the suspect guilty of the

---

[2] Njaka, E.N., *op. cit.* p. 46.

crime. What happens is that if a villager is suspected of being responsible for the death of another villager by poisoning or by any other occult means, the suspect would be required to swear before a powerful tutelar deity that he is innocent of the accusation. Usually, it is the accused who initiates the move to prove his innocence.

Even where there is substantial evidence and there are many witnesses to testify that the accused poisoned the deceased, the accused would be held innocent if he swears the oath. If the suspect swears his oath and no harm befalls him after a year or two he will be held acquitted by the supernatural tribune. It is a strong belief backed by considerable prodigies even if coincidental in Igbo traditional society, that if the accused were guilty of the crime, *Ani* and the ancestors would either kill him or inflict some grave punishment which may be blindness, leprosy, small-pox or a mass death of the accused relations. It is also held that some deities, like Nemesis, are slow-footed. This means that rather than immediately punishing the accused who swore falsely, the punishment may be deferred till much later in the perjurer's life or in some cases the punishment due to the perjurer may be transferred to his children or close relations. This is why swearing in Igboland is fraught with utmost danger. Usually, people do all they can to avoid it if it is avoidable. To cause a neighbour to swear for you is to perpetuate your enemity with him.

There is yet another option that may be followed in the case of suspected homicide by poisoning. In my locality, if a man is suspected to be responsible for the death of his relative, he would not be allowed to see the corpse of the deceased. If the feeling against the suspect is too tense, he would be made to drink of the water used in washing the deceased relation's body. He should drink this to prove his innocence. If he was really responsible for the death of the relative, he himself would die after some definite time but if he is innocent, nothing would happen to him. Here again the judgment is passed to a supernatural arbitration. Even in the case of incest, the same course is taken. Where there is no material evidence that the suspects committed the act, there would be recourse to a supernatural tribune in the form of swearing.

In contrast to the above, theft which is not regarded as *nsọ* and therefore not a breach of divine law but rather a violation of human law, is punished *eo instante*. If a man steals from a kinsman, *umunna*, during which the case is presented for hearing. The thief will be sternly warned besides being rebuked if what was stolen was a trifle. Otherwise, the thief is tied up for days without food; if he is caught red-handed he is carried about the village especially round the market squares, with the stolen property conspicuously tied around his neck while passers-by jeer, curse and spit on him. The thief is expected to make restitution.

A man suspected of theft is "put on trial" and if there is substantial evidence and the testimonies of the witnesses are consistently against him he will be convicted and punished appropriately. It stands clear from the foregoing that the field of divine laws in Igbo traditional set-up is exclusively supervised and administered by the supernatural whereas other laws are enacted, administered and enforced by the appropriate human institutions.

Furthermore, no violation of the divine laws would go unpunished. It is held by the Igbo that no *nso* behaviour, no *alu* (abomination) will escape the searching eyes of *Chukwu* even if the perpetrators have successfully concealed them from human eyes. The offenders must be punished either during their life time, or at the end of it or even during their next life cycle (reincarnation). What E. Adeotu Adegbola, a Nigerian writer says about African morality in general is relevant here:

> Everywhere African morality is hinged on many sanctions. But the most fundamental sanction is the fact that God's all-seeing eyes scan the total area of human behaviour and personal relationships. God is spoken of as having eyes all over like a sieve.[3]

In consequence of the Igbo belief in the inevitability of divine vengeance for the violation of divine laws, grave misfortunes are thought to be god-sent punishments. Thus, if lightning strikes a man or his house, it is seen as a punishment for some hidden crime committed by the victim. Sudden death is usually attributed to the same cause though evil spirit and evil men including sorcery are among the causes of such calamities. A person who died with a swollen stomach known as *afo-otito* is not usually buried in the village cemetery. The corpse is thrown into the *ajo ofia* the "evil forest" where evil men alone are buried for it is believed that it was the accumulation of his "crimes" that caused his "bad" death.

Uchendu agrees with this views in the following passage:

> ...the death of young people are usually blamed on the sins committed during their previous life on earth; deaths of adults may be attributed to "ripe" age, or senility, or a breach of taboo or other antisocial

---

[3] Adegbola, E.A., quoted by Onyewenyi, I., cf. *Readings In African Humanities, African Cultural Development*, ed. U.K. University of Nigeria, Nsukka, Enugu, 1978, p. 252.

behaviour, such as sorcery, false oath, or theft committed in his previous or present life. If sorcery is involved, the deceased adult is denied a "ground burial" (a privilege accorded only to those who die without blemish), and the corpse is cast into *ofia ojo* - "bad bush" fit only for the outcast. The ritual purifications are primarily designed to dissociate the living from the deceased's blemish and thus re-establish the ritual balance his breach of the taboo has destroyed.[4]

Only the violation of the divine laws, which violation is held as *nso* or *alu* could be regarded as a criminal offence to use western legal term. But it is something much more than a criminal offence strictly speaking.

When a "criminal" is not punished or adequately punished during his life time, the punishment is stored for him against his next life-time, that is when he reincarnates. Or he may never reincarnate which is perhaps the greatest punishment in the eyes of the traditional Igbo.

Another curious phenomena associated with the violation of the divine laws is the "confession at death bed".Practically all the notorious criminals in my village, men who were allegedly responsible for the untimely death of other villagers by either poisoning, sorcery or magic, have been said to have confessed their awful crimes at their death bed. Such men are usually known and feared in the society. And similar account of "confession at death bed" are recorded in other parts of Igboland. The criminal usually dies shortly after the confession. The confession is made to nobody in particular. The dying man normally recalls the awful deeds he had done to the hearing of everybody present. He then, draws his last breath. This writer has witnessed one such confession but I am inclined to think that the confession might have been precipitated by the mental condition of the dying man rather than by the supposed action of some supernatural force as the people believed. At any rate, this could be a very interesting case study for psychoanalysts.

So far in our discussion on the divine laws in the Igbo traditional context, I have pointed out the sense in which "divine" is used to qualify certain laws. Divine is used in contra-distinction from human. It is used not in the absolute sense but relatively. That certain laws are qualified as "divine" does not therefore mean that they are directly handed down to man in written commandments like the biblical Decalogue.

In the context of Igbo jurisprudence, the laws we have described as divine are by the fact of their fundamentality and their religious import

---

4 Uchendu, V.C., *op. cit.*, p. 13.

divine. In practical life, there is a conscious effort to avoid the violation of these laws not because of fear of any human institution but because they are believed to carry divine sanction, a supernatural sanction. Moreover, the violation of these laws is not only regarded as "criminal offence" but also it is considered irreligious. This religious aspect of these laws further stresses their divine nature. There is need for religious purification after each violation of these laws. We have spoken about this previously. Again, the punishment for the breach of these laws is believed to come ultimately from God.

Indeed, the laws which no human institution has the right to mitigate nor competent to try and punish the offender are certainly not human laws. They are obviously divine laws at least by implication.

The Igbo Concept of Divine Justice

Our discussion on the divine laws viewed from the Igbo traditional perspective brings another question to the fore-the question of the nature of divine justice in Igbo traditional thought.

Generally, the Igbo seek and cherish justice in all spheres of human activities. An unjust man is looked upon with contempt and disregard and is never allowed to hold any serious social position. The Igbo idea of justice is clear and distinct. For them, justice simply means - giving to everyone what is his due. Favouritism in any gender or case stands condemned as a mutilation of justice. There must be equal reward or punishment for equal merit or offence. But the Igbo notice that absolute justice is not possible in any human society. Hence, in vital issues they seek the redress of divine justice. In Igbo traditional concept, divine justice has the following characteristics:

1. It is absolute.
2. It is impartial though capricious.
3. It is immutable.
4. It is not bound by space and time.

Man is always in quest of the absolute which is always invariably found in God. Since the Igbo perceive that human justice is not absolute and yet stand in need of absolute justice, they believe that only God can administer such justice. Thus, in the Igbo traditional legal system, the highest court of appeal is the supernatural tribunal. When all the · recognised Igbo judicial institutions have failed to resolve a dispute to the satisfaction of the injured party, the final option is seek redress from the supernatural which alone can dispense absolute, pure and final justice. This might take the form of swearing or consulting an oracle.

When one party in a legal dispute swears an oath to testify to the truth of his claims, the other party will be satisfied to withdraw his own claims with utter resignation believing that God will not fail to vindicate the cause of justice. The claimant, if he swore falsely must be punished appropriately to the satisfaction of the other party that divine justice has prevailed. From the concept of the absolute nature of divine justice arises the idea of the impartiality of divine justice. The human judicial institutions could be trusted only up to a point. This is why people could decline to accept the judgment passed by any of the traditional judicial institutions. But any judgment passed by the supernatural tribunes is unquestionably acceptable to all parties concerned no matter how sour the judgment may taste. This is because divine judgment is held to be impartial, hence divine justice too.

On the other hand, the fact that the same offence is punishable in different ways by (God) the supernatural seems to suggest that God is capricious. For instance, if two persons committed *nso* or *alu* of the same nature, one may die as a consequence, the other may be inflicted with some deadly disease like leprosy. One would expect a uniform punishment for the same offence for all persons if the impartiality of divine justice is to be absolute. Here, the Igbo are not much concerned with the nature of the punishment suffered by a "criminal". They are concerned rather with the fact that the offender has been adequately punished for his *nso* or *alu* (abomination). Obviously, his trust in the impartiality of divine justice overrides the above apparent contradiction.

Next is the immutability of divine justice. The Igbo conceive divine justice as constant and changeless. Of course this is a logical consequence of the Igbo belief in the immutability of divine will. This short Igbo tale illustrates this belief and concept.

> Once upon a time, in the beginning of things, man sent the tortoise to God to deliver a petition to Him. The petition was that man might remain immortal on earth. After some time, man's enemy sent a dog with a contrary petition - that man should not remain immortal on earth. Because the tortoise is a slow animal, the dog out-ran him on the way and appeared and presented the contrary petition to God. God accepted the petition. Later the tortoise arrived with the petition from man but it was already too late. God had decreed that man must die and could not change his mind. This is why man is not immortal on earth.

This story has many versions in Igboland but in each version the idea of the immutability of divine will is sufficiently stressed.

Time and space do not affect divine justice. It is within the reach of all people and all time. It is this concept of the impartiality of divine justice as well as its transcendental nature that make the Igbo believe that one's merits, one's achievements, one's social status shall be maintained in the "hereafter", that is in the spirit world.

Emerging from our discussion on the concept of divine law and divine justice in Igbo traditional thought is the conclusion that divine justice and divine mercy follow opposite directions. Violation of the divine laws are not pardonable. Repentance of the "sinner" does not absolve him from nor mitigates in any way the punishment. Where then is the place of divine mercy?

The Igbo concept of divine mercy is very obscure. When things are going wrong with him, he does not simply pray God to change the course of the event or to have mercy on him for an apparent offence he committed. He usually seeks for a way out of the situation which may be *ichu aja* - ritual sacrifice. He believes that he can wriggle out of his situation by negotiating with the spirit which might be responsible for his plight. He does not usually hope to change his situation by merely imploring God's mercy.

Besides the divine laws, there are other categories of law identifiable in the unsystematised Igbo laws. The next to be considered are the natural laws both in their conceptual and practical forms.

The Natural Law viewed from the traditional Igbo Perspective

Perhaps, the heated controversy which swept across the western world over the centuries concerning the natural law might have been occasioned by the misconceptions and misapplication of the word *nature* in relation to laws. Before we proceed to examine the concept of the natural law against the Igbo traditional legal background we must first of all examine the concept in its restricted sense and meaning.

Now the term nature, to begin with is used in a great variety of meanings. Sometimes it is used to designate the material universe; thus, when we speak of a thing "existing in nature", we mean that it is to be found in the bodily world around us. Again, nature is often used to designate all bodily beings except man, and in contrast with man; and here, in particular it means living creatures although it does not exclude lifeless things. Again, nature is used to designate man as contrasted with other bodily things; it is used in the sense of human nature. Ethymologically, the term nature is derived from the latin participle *natus* - "born", a form of the verb *nascive* "to be born". And the nature of things suggests what the things are born for; what they are originated to do; what they exist to accomplish.

Now, the natural order obviously obey the natural law or the law of nature. In so far as the law which governs creatures is understood as the decree of the Creator, it may be called Eternal law - eternal because being an ordinance of divine wisdom, it is changeless and timeless. It governs all creatures, bodily and spiritual. But it governs man through his reason; it governs him by suasion. The same law governs natural bodies by necessitation.

In so far as the Eternal law is recognised by sound human reason in the domain of man's free conduct, it is called the natural law. On the other hand, in so far as the Eternal Law stands manifested in the regular and harmonious activities of the bodies, it is called the law of nature. Thus, the natural law is one unique law which may further split into moral law when it applies to man as a rational and moral being, and physical law when it applies to other bodies. The dispute over the natural law arises not in its application to the physical bodies as physical laws but in its application to man as moral laws. I shall examine the natural law in all its extensions in order to show that the concept is latent in Igbo traditional thought.

The natural law as we have shown above, is the ordinance of Divine Wisdom by which the entire creatures are governed. The law is latent in nature. Man is able to discover it through the operation of his reason. But being endowed with a free will he may choose to obey or disobey the law. Now, since the law is latent in nature and is discoverable by human reason, it follows that men have been living in accordance with the dictates of this law over the ages without necessarily knowing the law by any specific name. Thus, the natural law is only a concept which explains certain realities in the moral and physical order.

In our discussion on the Igbo concept of divine law, we pointed out that one of the characteristics of this law is that it is not traceable to any historical source. I explained that the Igbo obey them without knowing and bothering to know from whence they come. I drew attention to the fact that this inability by the Igbo to trace the divine laws to any historical source also portrays these laws as the natural law, because they are discovered by reason alone.

Homicide, for instance, is held as a taboo. Killing a human being is a breach of the divine law. The punishment for such an abominable offence is reserved solely to the supernatural, because it is seen as an offence directly against God. But there was no point in time when this law is known to have been promulgated in any form whatsoever. Thus, homicide besides being forbidden by the divine law is also contrary to the natural law. It is obvious that the Igbo discovered through the operation of his reason that homicide is against the ordinance of God. But the natural law is but the Ordinance of God as discovered by mere human reason. Hence the concept of the natural law is latent in Igbo traditional thought.

Again, incest, defined as sexual intercourse with a person one cannot marry by reason of their blood relationship, is a taboo. It is an abomination, a violation of the divine law. Persons who committed incest are sold into slavery because they are thought to have polluted the land, *iru ala* - in other words, they have violated the order of the natural law. The fact that the Igbo conscientiously avoid all *nso* behaviours not because they are forbidden by any statutes nor because they are forbidden by "God's commandments" (the traditional Igbo do not know of any God's written commandments) further illustrates the fact that the concept of the natural law is latent in the Igbo traditional thought. The conclusion is that like all other people of the world, the Igbo have been living in accordance with the dictates of the natural law and making their laws in the light of the natural law principles without even knowing or using the term, "natural law". I have tried to show that the concept of the natural law in its restricted sense is also latent in Igbo traditional thought.

In the widest sense of the word, the natural law has been variously defined, interpreted and applied. There is yet another sense in which the natural law could be understood in the Igbo context. This other meaning would certainly make more sense to an Igbo villager more than the natural law in its restricted sense which is more or less an abstract concept.

Ani, the earth, is believed by the Igbo to be a goddess. The earth-goddess and *Chukwu*, the supreme Being, are jointly responsible for creation. In reply to the question posed by Rev. Arazu, Ezenwadeyi, an elder of Ihembosi among other things affirmed:

> ...It is *Chukwu* and this earth (*Ana*)
> On which we stand
> They, we are told,
> Own all men
> Who put the hand into the mouth
> And all the trees
> And each

And everything;
It is the same *Chukwu*
And this *Ana* (Earth)
Who brought out man and put him up;
We are not witnesses
We are saying
What we were told.

Here the joint action of God and the earth goddess in creation is once again emphasized.

Now, certain offences as we have seen already are regarded as against *Ana* or *Ala*, the earth and the perpetrators of such offences are said to have polluted the earth - "*Ha merulu ala*". "Polluting the earth" here must be understood as disrupting the natural order. This is why a purification ritual must be performed after each breach of taboo in order to restore the natural order that has been upset. As a concept, *Ani* or *ala* represent the totality of nature. And to violate its law is to violate the natural law. Thus, the laws of *ala* are the laws of nature. Coincidently, we have shown that all *nso* or *alu* are violations of the divine law which have been shown to be by implication the natural law.

In the widest sense of the word, therefore, the natural law in Igbo traditional concept would comprise all those laws the violation of which are regarded as offence against the earth which represent the totality of nature. This law governs not only man but also other creatures as we shall see shortly.

The natural law governs not only man but also other creatures. Obviously a traditional Igbo is not aware of the law of relativity which is the natural law in a physical order. Nor is he familiar with the law of gravity. But he is certainly aware of the fact that other creatures living and non living, other than man, are subject to some law, the law of nature. I shall illustrate.

There are certain phenomena which the Igbo regard as out of tune with the natural order, that is to say contrary to the law of nature. In a typical village in Igbo land, if a cock crows at an odd hour, say at the midnight, that cock must be killed by the owner. Such a cock is thought to be "bad" cock because it is acting contrary to its nature, contrary to the law of nature which require it to crow only at certain time of the day namely early in the morning and at regular intervals during the day.

In a typical Igbo traditional society, cock crow is used to measure the time of the day. The first cock crow marks the dawn of the day.

Cock crow is also used to mark the mid-day. Apart from the cock crow, the position of the sun is another way of measuring the time of the day in a typical Igbo society. Now, the cock crow is adopted as a measure of time, because the Igbo observed that it follows a regular natural order. It is no wonder that any deviation from this natural regularity is seen as contrary to the natural order, to the law of nature.

An Igbo proverb says: "*Awo anaghi agba oso ehihe na nkiti*" meaning, literally, that toad does not run about in the daylight without a cause". The toad is a nocturnal animal and it is its nature to come out only in the night. If however, you see a toad on the run in a broad day light, certainly something is wrong somewhere. This shows that the toad will not normally run about during the day without a cause otherwise it will be acting contrary to its nature, contrary to the law of nature which is ultimately the eternal law or the divine law.

Any violation of the natural law or the law of nature either by man or other creatures carries grave consequences in Igbo traditional society. A man who committed homicide must hang himself. Persons guilty of incest are sold into slavery. A cock which crows at an odd time contrary to the known law of its nature is killed by the Igbo. All this portrays the fundamentality of the law of nature.

We have been able to show that the concept of the law of nature or the natural law in the strictest sense of the phrase, is latent in the Igbo traditional thought. In the widest sense of the phrase, the Igbo regard the natural law as concrete laws valid for men and other creatures, laws which man or any creature could violate only to his or its detriment.

Moral Laws

The moral law, as a concept, understood as the natural law which regulates rational human conduct is latent in Igbo traditional thought. But moral law conceived as distinct from the divine or the natural law, and taken to be a set of rules designed to direct man's conduct is entirely alien to Igbo thought. This is so because morality and religion overlap in Igbo traditional society. There is in fact no term for morality in Igbo language. And thus, the concept of moral laws as such is foreign to Igbo thoughts.

In a typical Igbo society, an act is bad either because it offends God or the ancestors or because it is contrary to *Omenala* (law and customs of the land). So the Igbo would always ask whether his action is in keeping with *Omenala* and not whether his action is moral or not. And *Omenala* forbids all those actions which are ontologically evil and promotes the good ones. This is a caveat for a hasty conclusion that the Igbo have no morality. For after all, *Omenala* the Igbo constitution provides explicit norms of good and evil which may be called moral code.

On African ethical life in general, Innocent Onyewuenyi observed that:

> The norms of good and evil are objective and of universal validity; no room exists for subjectivism or solipsism and situational ethics. African ethical truths are not relative. Except for cases of ignorance, there are few if any mitigating circumstances.[5]

This observation made by an Igbo scholar and philosopher is very true of Igbo morality.

Igbo Human Positive Laws

Legal rules are of two main classes and are recognised as such. There are those which might be called ordinary human laws and those whose breach is held to be not only illegal but also an offence against the supernatural. So far, our attention has been focused on those laws whose breach is held to be not only illegal but also an offence against the supernatural. In what follows, our discussion will be centred on the Igbo positive laws.

The Igbo make laws on a wide range of subjects including economic, social and political matters. Though the Igbo do not have a permanent legislative body or a specialised legal institution with powers to make laws, laws are nevertheless made by an ad hoc general assembly, *oha*, which is in fact an all purpose assembly. Whether in the making of laws affecting the wider Igbo political unit, the village-group (*Obodo*), or in the enactment of laws affecting a smaller political unit, village (*Ogbe*), the legislative procedures are much the same. Let us first examine the Igbo laws relating to economic matters.

The laws relating to economic matters may be in respect of the use of market places or in respect of the ownership and control of certain economic trees and common natural resources such as lakes and streams that provide fishes for home consumption and for the market.

In many Igbo villages, laws are made prohibiting women from going to the farms on market days. In the traditional society, every

---

5 Onyewuenyi, I., *"Towards an African Philosophy" Readings in African Humanities, African Cultural Development*, ed. Ogbu, U.K., U.N.N. 1978, p. 252.

village-group has a specific market day in which there is a large turn out of sellers and buyers from the village-group and its neigbours. The market day falls on every *izu* (the Igbo week of four days). Such law is intended to ensure that the market is well attended. A town's importance and popularity may depend simply on the strength of its market. The Anthropologist Green, who lived in Umuneke village in the heart of Igboland writes:

> One Orie Ekpa market day a number of people told me that a law had been made that all men and women of Agbaja must go regularly to Orie Ekpa market or be fined, because the people of Agbaja wanted their market to be big.[6]

Palm tree is a very important economic tree in Igboland. It yields oil for home consumption and for the market. Almost every part of the palm tree is useful to an Igboman - its kernels are used to feed the fire, its timber used in building houses, the fronds for covering mud walls against rain, its tender shoots serve as candles when dried and soaked in oil and as a source of the palm-wine which is the typical wine in Igboland.

It is no wonder therefore that laws are made regulating the use of the palm trees, which laws of course vary from village to village according to local economic circumstances. In my own village, the law permits the individual to cut palm nuts indiscriminately so long as the palm tree is not within somebody's compound. In some other villages, the law forbids the individual to cut palm nuts or palm fronds that are not in his land.

In the same way, indiscriminate fishing in common lakes or rivers are forbidden by law in some areas of Igboland. Fishing in such lakes or rivers is allowed only at a fixed time of the year and the entire community is involved during the fishing festival. This law is common in the Igbo coastal towns of Anam, Aguleri and Mmiata to mention but a few. People who violate these laws are made to pay appropriate fines.

There are also laws which are principally intended to give social directives. Such laws concern the use and maintenance of public social facilities such as roads, village squares, springs etc. Roads are constructed and maintained by the villagers. The major roads are those leading to the market places, to the farms, to the springs or streams from where the villagers fetch drinking water and roads connecting the town to other neighbouring village-groups. The law requires every male

---

[6] Green, M.M., *op. cit.* p. 134.

adult to participate in the maintenance of these roads whenever they are called upon. Any adult male who fails to show up on the fixed day for the community work must have to pay some fine.

The maintenance of village springs or streams as the case may be is solely the duty of the womenfolk. Since the springs and the streams are the main sources of drinking water in the villages, due care is taken to ensure that their surroundings are kept clean. To this effect, the village women organise themselves in groups and each group will take its turn in cleaning the spring and its surroundings. In this way the spring is cleaned and maintained every week. Anyone who fails to participate in this work is liable to pay a fine. The women could also make bye-laws giving directives on what must be done by all users of the spring to keep it clean.

Some years ago, there was a popular law known as "*iwu oku*". It was first enacted in one town but later other village groups followed suit. The *iwu oku* required the individual to carry a bush lamp or a lantern if he is moving about the village at night. This law was intended to check the activities of thieves and other evil doers who roam about village in the night. In any village where this law was in force, an age-grade was detailed to 'enforce' it.

There are also laws which relate to political matters. Laws are made concerning the political relationship of one village-group and another. Some village-groups are known to have made laws forbidding their citizens from attending the market of their neighbouring village group for political reasons. Boundary disputes are among the most common causes of the break down in diplomatic relationships between Igbo city states. There are other causes such as the molestation of members of one village-group by another. At any event, if for any reason a law is made boycotting the market of another village-group, to go contrary to such law has grave consequences. The offender is usually made to pay a heavy fine.

Not only are new laws made to meet the needs of changing social, political and economic situations, but also old laws are subject to amendment or total abrogation. Very recently, most Igbo villages passed a law prohibiting the riding of motorcycles in the villages during the major feasts of the year. The law was intended to prevent alarming incidents of motor-cycle accidents which are caused by drunken motor-cyclists during the feasts.

When a law is no longer effective either because it has outlived its usefulness or because it is no longer popular, that law is shelved by a series of quiet evasions. Under the Igbo legislative system with many checks and balances, a tyranical law is just not possible. This remark will be further substantiated in the following chapter.

The laws adumbrated above are positive laws as such and are clearly distinct from customs. This distinction is recognised by the Igbo both in theory and in practice. The breaking of any of these laws mentioned above may call forth action, ultimately backed by some kind of force or sanction, on the part of, or endorsed by the community. Ordinary customary rules are not enforceable and their breach is not illegal.

I have merely been exposing the Igbo human positive laws. They are not in any way exhausted here. And my intention is not to compile the whole lot of Igbo positive laws into one volume. However, this brief exposition will enable us to see the contrast between the laws whose breach are held to be *nso* (taboo) which laws I have classified as divine laws and ordinary human laws which deal specifically with social, economic and political matters. But we have to bear in mind that the Igbo religion permeates all facets of Igbo life - social, political and even economic. We shall be considering later the impact of the Igbo religion on their positive laws.

So far, I have attempted to analyse the main sectors of Igbo laws which are scattered legal rules. An attempt has also been made to classify these laws in a most comprehensible form in the light of universal legal principles. Emerging from our discussion are the following points about the Igbo laws in general:

1.   Divine laws are clearly distinguished from ordinary human laws.
2.   Divine laws supercede the human laws and where there arises a conflict between the demands of the two laws, that of the divine law shall prevail.
3.   The Igbo laws are effective instrument for achieving social harmony, promoting moral rectitude and maintaining sound political order.

In the next chapter of this work, we shall closely examine the main features of Igbo human positive laws. The indigenous values of Igbo legal system will be highlighted and critically assessed at the same time.

Chapter 4

The Characteristic Features Of Igbo Positive Laws

It is necessary at this point to examine the essential features of Igbo positive laws with a view to highlighting their inner values and at the same time identifying the unchanging principles that form the basis of all Igbo man made law in general. Now for any piece of legislation to qualify as law in Igbo traditional society, it must:

1. Bear a stamp of legitimacy
2. Pass the test of reasonableness
3. Be sufficiently promulgated
4. Be intended for the common good
5. And must not be contrary to the established custom (*Omenala*).

We shall proceed to examine each of the above mentioned features in the light of Igbo concrete legal situations.

Legitimacy

No Igbo positive law is binding unless it bears a stamp of legitimacy. By this I mean that for any piece of legislation to acquire the force of law, it must be known as proceeding from the right authoritative source. This is evident from the rigorous legislative process through which a law must pass before it is declared and adopted as such in Igbo society.

That the Igbo have no permanent legislative body or assembly nor a legislative house as is known in the western world does not mean that laws are arbitrarily made perhaps, by some powerful capricious elements in Igbo country. This is far from being the reality. There are well defined and recognised legislative processes through which a law must pass before it carries a mark of authority. What the British Anthropologist, Green says is relevant here:

> There seems to be no specialised institution for this function and one meets again the fact that a group of people met together for some economic purpose such as a market or some traditional purpose such as a second burial will use the occasion of meeting to discuss public matters. It is as though the *res publica* were only gradually emerging from the sphere of kinship.

to discover, this is not to say that the Ibo do not make and proclaim laws - *iti iwu*.[1]

To a westerner, already familiar with western legislative process, the Igbo traditional legislative process would seem informal. And this is what Green expressed above while admitting that the Igbo nevertheless make and proclaim laws.

Now, the legislative authority rests with the *Oha*, the village general assembly and the legitimacy of any law derives there from. All adult males meeting in ad hoc general assembly, *Oha*, have full rights to participate in the legislative activity. Occasional meetings like that are held in the village open square or in the market place. Nowadays, village halls are preferred. When the meeting is thus in session, a legislative move could be initiated by any body or group. Then the matter is thrown open for discussion. Anybody who has an opinion to express on the matter is given a hearing. When all possible views on the matters have been heard, the heads from each lineage in the village retire for a "close session". The right to participate in this "consultative session" called *izuzu*, is reserved to men with high esteem and good moral reputation having sufficient wisdom to discern the direction of public opinion. At the end of the *izuzu* session, a spokesman, usually a very eloquent fellow from the group announces the decision. If the final decision is acceptable to the *Oha*, the general assembly, the decision will be greeted with general acclamation otherwise it is rejected with shouts of disapproval. Invariably, the view and will of the *Oha* shall prevail. V.C. Uchendu remarked that:

> The Igbo are jealous of their legislative authority and are not willing to surrender it to a small group of individuals.[2]

Now, the second phase of the legislative process is the "ritual endorsement of the law". When a piece of legislation has been thus proclaimed into law by the *Oha*, the *Ọfọ* holders will ratify it by invoking this formula:

> "This *iwu* (law) is in accordance with our custom and must be obeyed and respected. Those who refuse to obey the law, may *Ọfọ* kill them".

Each time the *Ọfọ* is struck on the ground (usually four times), the *Oha* assents *ise* or *iha* meaning "let it be so". The law is then made known to the entire village through the male adults and householders whose

---

[1] Green, M.M., *op. cit*. p. 132.

[2] Uchendu V.C. *op. cit*. 42.

responsibility it is to explain the legislation further to the members of their respective families.

It is important to note that some major Igbo institutionalised societies may initiate legislative move and win the day if they secure enough public support. The most popular of these include age grade society, the *dibia* fraternity, the *amala* or *ndichie* and the *Ọkọnkọ* society. Green also observed that:

A group such as the *ndi dibia* or age group can take the (legislative) initiative and win the day if they secure enough public support.

In all cases, the *Oha*, the people's assembly, is the ultimate legislative authority and the only source of any legitimate law in Igbo community. Thus from the foregoing, it is evident that legitimacy is an essential feature of Igbo positive laws. Any law which does not bear this stamp of legitimacy which derives from the people loses its validity and its power to bind. Such a law is gradually shelved by series of quiet evasions.

Granted that the Igbo laws are characterised by their legitimacy, are they also firmly established on sound rationality or are they product of mass hysteria of Igbo general assembly called *Oha*? This is the second feature of the Igbo positive laws that must be examined.

The Igbo Laws as Ordinances of Reason

The primary question here is whether the Igbo laws, as rules of human conduct, are ethically sound by being fair, just, honest and morally possible to observe. A law which is impossible to observe is certainly not a reasonable law for instead of being an ordinance of reason for common good it becomes an ordinance of un-reason for common detriment. Nevertheless, such laws are enacted and enforced in many parts of the globe.

Evidently, the law-making process in Igbo society does not make room for an unreasonable law. This is because, as we have seen previously, legislative activities are open to everybody. No individual or group of persons have a right to impose a law on the Igbo. The entire people, as it were, that is, the *Oha*, are involved in the law-making. Thus, Igbo laws are not the product of the reason of one individual as in authocratic states nor that of a group of people as in aristocratic system nor even that of the so called representatives of the people as in modern democratic set-ups, but the product of the reason of the people themselves, such as in the "Ohacratic" state of the Igbo, a system reminiscent of the Greek City States. In fact,

---

3 Green, M.M. *op. cit.* p. 137.

unreasonable law is not enactable in "Ohacratic" legislative system, for the people themselves cannot make a law which is impossible for them to observe.

By the same token, fairness and honesty are the guiding principle in the Igbo "Ohacratic state" where the law is made by the people for the people. For the people to make an unfair and unjust law for themselves will tantamount to selves-deceit. Thus the Igbo "Ohacracy" and the unique legislative process ensure that any piece of legislation must have a reasonable foundation, and be fair, just, honest and easily observable by the law abiding.

We may briefly look at one or two Igbo pieces of legislation to see if they pass the test of reasonableness. The *iwu oku* (the light law) may serve our purpose. The *iwu oku* is a law which states that every person walking about the village in the night must carry a bush lamp or lantern or in fact any form of light but not torch light. This law was not intended to restrict the people's freedom of movement nor is it a curfew. The law rather aims at the protection of the property of the people. Of course, the background of this law justifies its aim.

Before the enactment of this law, there was growing number of cases of theft in the villages. Coincidentally, there were reports of missing people believed to have been kidnapped by evil men who make powerful medicines and magic. In Ibo country, thieves seldom operate in the day time and kidnappers waylay their victims mainly during the night. The *iwu oku* was therefore made to check the activities of the thieves and kidnappers.

In Igbo traditional villages there are no street lights and it is difficult to identify anybody in the dark of the night. The *iwu oku*, requiring the individual to carry a lamp or a lantern, is the only safe way by which the identity of anybody would be known in the dark of the night. Anybody found loitering about the village in the dark of the night without a light might be suspected reasonably of having the intention to execute some dark design. Such a person is called to question or may be required to pay an appropriate fine for the breach of the law. Thus, the rationality, the fairness and the ethical soundness of this law is glaringly evident.

If we further consider any Igbo law relating to economic issue, the same rational principle would be seen to characterise it. Take, for instance, the law forbidding people to go to the farms on market days. This law, viewed from a narrow perspective, would seem unjust and unfair as it appears to interfere with the people's fundamental right to choose freely from a set of alternative legitimate economic activities. But viewed from a broader perspective, with an eye on the main objective of that law, it is fair, just and ethically sound through and through.

An Igbo village economy depends largely on what it can produce and sell. The market is very vital in the Ibo economy because it is the only medium for all local economical activities and the major source through which the village obtains its "Foreign exchange". For the village economy to grow, therefore, its market must be viable, capable of attracting "foreign" business men and women. The volume of business activities in any given market naturally depends on the population of the market. For this reason every village strives to attract buyers from other villages by ensuring that its market square is full to the capacity each market day. An empty market may be a sign of weakness on the part of the village. The law is made forbidding the villagers from going to the farms on the market day to ensure that people turn out in large numbers for the market. If the village loses its market because of poor attendance, its economy suffers and this will be followed by a series of economic consequences culminating in serious economic and social distress.

On the surface, therefore, "the market day law" may seem unfair and unjust but when one probes the law a layer further, the law will be seen as ethically sound and reasonable. Logically, the short run interests of the individual villagers who may wish to go to the farm on the market day should not overide the collective interests of the village on the long run. The village's collective interest or common good is to have a viable economy which only a popular market can procure in the Igbo economic order.

The Igbo positive laws are indeed ordinances of reason. We have established this fact about the Igbo laws with reference to the singular legislative process of the people. We have shown that "Ohacracy" does not tolerate unjust and unfair legislation. And, finally, we have examined concrete pieces of Igbo legislation and found them to be fair, just, honest and morally possible to observe.

The Laws must be Promulgated

Once a given piece of legislation has undergone the legislative processes already described above, and is finally proclaimed a law, the next essential stage is to promulgate the law, to bring it to the notice of the public. Without promulgation, the process of law making is not considered as completed by the Igbo. A law that is not known by the generality of the Igbo village public may be regarded as non-existent.

A law is not regarded as promulgated in Igbo country merely because it has been entered into the gazette. Publication of laws in the government's official media is altogether an unfamiliar method of disseminating news or legal enactments in the Igbo "Ohacracy". Besides, in the Igbo "ohacratic" government, the above methods would be considered inadequate as means of promulgating laws.

There are two efficient means of bringing a new law to the knowledge of the village public, which is what promulgation essentially means - making a piece of legislation known. Law-making as we have pointed out earlier on is a public affair in Igbo country. Everyone, especially the adult males are free to participate. Usually, legislative activities are carried out during occasional meetings when practically all the menfolk of the village are in attendance. This means that virtually all the *umunna* are represented by their *paterfamiliae*. When eventually a piece of legislation is proclaimed into law and ratified by the *Ọfọ* holders, it becomes the civic duty of every *paterfamiliae* and householder not only to bring the new law to the knowledge of his family or household but also to explain the legislation to the members of his family and see to it that his family obeys the law. In this way every family in the village or village-group comes to know the new law. This is one Igbo way of promulgating a law.

Another effective method of promulgating a new law is by the agency of the village or "town crier". Every village or town has an "announcer" (town crier) whose exclusive function it is to disseminate information to the entire village or town. A "town crier" is carefully selected from among the people. He must possess a powerful and sonorous voice capable of arousing and captivating the attention of the public.

Now, when a new law is made, the "crier" is commissioned to go around the village to announce it with the penalties or sanctions carried by the breach of the law well outlined. To make sure that the announcement gets to the hearing of everybody, the announcer usually goes around the village during the night or very early in the morning. First, he would strike his *ogene* or *ekwe* (metal gong or wooden gong) to call the attention of the people. Then in a clear, distinct masculine and sonorous pitch of voice, he announces the new legislation. At the end of each announcement he concludes with these words:

I have announced to you what I have been commissioned to announce.

Having said this, he would strike his metal or wooden gong once again and then proceeds to another part of the village or town.

The announcer must not fail to reach every part of the town or the village as the case may be.

According to the implied provision of the Igbo legislative system, a piece of legislation acquires the force of law only after it has been so promulgated by either of the two methods described above. Invariably, the latter is employed to complement the former. Thus, promulgation is an' essential feature of Igbo positive laws. And the Igbo adopts the most efficient and the most effective methods in promulgating their law. Such methods are in fact practicable in the "Ohacratic" system of Igbo government.

In a traditional Igbo judicial system, non culpable ignorance is an excuse in the man-made laws. If a man violates a law clearly out of ignorance and the ignorance is not due to his fault, he is acquitted on that ground. By the same token, a foreigner who violates any of the Igbo positive laws out of ignorance can be excused. This consideration emphasizes a very important attitude of the Igbo towards the law, and that is this-the Igbo respect and obey the spirit of the law and not just its letters. Law is not regarded as a stumbling block for common detriment but as rules and regulations designed to preserve the peace, harmony and security of the community at large.

On the whole, we have shown that though unwritten and "unpublished" the Igbo laws are nevertheless duly promulgated. The peculiar methods of promulgating a law have been discussed - methods which are only workable in an "Ohacratic" system of the Igbo government. Above all, it emerged clearly from our discussion that promulgation is an essential feature of Igbo positive laws and no law is valid until it has been adequately made known to the public.

Common Good: The Goal of Igbo Laws

Every Igbo positive law must cut across individual or sectional interests otherwise, it would not qualify as law in the first place. For any piece of legislation to be proclaimed into law, it must be seen clearly as intended for the common good. Retrospective laws are hard to find in Igbo society.

The Igbo legislative system which is founded on the principle of "Ohacracy" makes it absolutely impossible for any piece of legislation with sectional bias to be enacted into a law. The Igbo legislative system provides that no individual or group of individuals could make laws to the exclusion of others. In principle and in practice every adult male in the village is a legislator. The village general assembly, *Oha*, is also a legislative assembly. When and where it meets, legislative activities could take place and everybody takes an active part. A proposed piece of legislation is placed before the assembly for consideration and possible adoption. Everybody who has a view to express on the matter is given a hearing. When all shades of opinion have been heard on the issue, a selected few, mainly people who are held in high esteem and with sufficient wisdom to discern where the "public opinion" lies amidst the various hues of views expressed will retire into an "*izuzu* session" (consultative session). The decision which is then announced after this "*izuzu* session" is in no way final. The assembly will react either in favour or out of favour of the decision if the decision is welcomed by the assembly, it will be acclaimed by shouts of approval, otherwise it will be rejected with shouts of disapproval. The public opinion must always prevail. The legislative process in Igboland is very rigorous. Most times an acceptable decision may not be reached at one session alone. When that happens the meeting is adjourned and a new date fixed for another.

The tediousness of Igbo legislative process is a direct result of their legislative objective - to ensure that the law so made is solely in the interest of common good. The law which virtually all the members of the community took part in the making cannot at the same time be against the common interest and good of the same community. The absence of political parties with warring ideologies in Igbo "Ohacracy" is a positive political reality for it enables the individuals to speak truly, freely and honestly on a given issue without reference to party ideals and pursuits. This means that during a legislative deliberations, people speak without bias or sectional interest in mind. The law that is finally adopted cannot but be for the common good.

If time or other human circumstances push a law to a point where it is seen no longer to be for the common good, that law would either be amended or revoked. This was exactly the situation at Umuneke village where an old law had to be amended because time and circumstances had made it unpopular and had given rise to resentments in a section of the village. Here, I shall reproduce verbatim what M. M. Green who conducted a research among the Igbo village, Umuneke wrote:

> The important question of the right to cut palm nuts was regulated one market day in Umuneke. The prevailing system, which had already replaced another before I arrived, was that people might only cut from palms on the land belonging to their own small land-owing group. This favoured the older men whose strength would not have allowed them to profit fully from a right to cut over a wider area, but did not suit the younger men. It was from one of these, J., that I heard about the change in the law. He was my next-door neighbour and a strong minded and independent young man. On the evening of one Umuneke market day he came to my house looking cock-a-

hoop and said that he and his age-group - *ebiri* had gone that afternoon in the market to the age group of the elders of the village and had made them alter the "law" about cutting palm nuts. The young men, he said, had insisted that hence forward palm nuts should be cut in general, each cutting where he liked, and, the younger men being numerous, they had borne down the opposition of the elders...As time went on one noticed that a compromise had apparently been reached in this question of cutting palm nuts and that the right to cut, though not entirely communal, was less restricted than before.[4]

We can easily see from the actual situation described above that an Igbo law which ceases to be an ordinance of reason for the common good must be amended. In the case narrated above, the young people of the community felt that the law did not cater for their interest. A strong delegation of the youth, styled the *ebiri* had to go and meet the council of the village elders to pour out their resentments. The youths prevailed over them at that instance. But the law was finally amended in the interest of common good when eventually a compromise point was reached in which the cutting of the palm nut, "though not entirely communal, was less restricted than before".

What is remarkable here is that the apparent conflict between the youths and the elders on the issue of the law regulating the cutting of palm nut was not resolved by the use of force nor by intimidation. When the youths met the village elders, who themselves are highly respected in Igbo society, the elders had agreed in principle to have the law amended. The law was finally amended not entirely in the interest of the youths to the exclusion of other vested interests. Rather the law was amended in such a way that the interest of the youth was adequately catered for while the overall interest of the community was in no way sacrificed. Thus the law was amended at the point of compromise, at the point where the common good of the people was achieved. It is obvious therefore that the common good is the goal of Igbo positive laws.

"Ohacentrism"

The major point to be borne in mind is that *Oha*, the entire people or the general assembly of the people as a body politic, is the yardstick for measuring the effectiveness and the legitimacy of any Igbo positive law. Every piece of legislation must emanate from the *Oha* the people and must be for the common good of the people. The *Oha*, is in fact a kind of social gyroscope so to say, preventing all other Igbo human institution especially

---

4 Green, M.M. *op. cit.* pp. 133-4.

the legal institution from deviating from their noble objectives which are to secure the peace, harmony, happiness and the good of the people.

The Igbo express their practical recognition of the supremacy of the law made by the *Oha*, in some of their traditional names. A very popular Igbo name that comes to mind is *"Iwuoha"*, meaning the "people's law". The name *"Iwuoha"* implies that the people's law must be obeyed because it is for the good of the people. *"Iwuoha"* the people's law must be fair, honest, ethically sound and anchored on the unshakable pillars of justice.

Again, the supremacy of *Oha*, the people's assembly over any individual or groups of individual is a living concept every Igboman deeply acknowledges. This is expressed in another Igbo name - *"Oraka"* - (*Oha* is supreme) the people's assembly is supreme. In other words the interest of the people as a body overides individual or sectional interest. To emphasise his awareness that the interest of the people, *Oha*, must come first and that the *Oha* has the power to overule in all cases, the Igbo say *"Orakwe"*, meaning if the people consent. *"Orakwe"* is also a typical Igbo name which means exactly what it reads.

My contention here is that in the typical Igbo social set-up the people's affairs whether executive, judicial or legislative, revolve round the *Oha* - the people themselves. This is what I mean by "Ohacentrism" - *Oha*-centred. And the logical consequence of this social atmosphere is that tyrannical laws are not enactible because of the rigid checks and balances; favoritism or sectionalism, twin social diseases which pervert justice are not thrivable in the political climate; and Ohacentrism promises the greatest happiness for the greatest number.

So far, we have demonstrated with sufficient facts and examples that Igbo positive laws are ordinances of reason, in each and all cases intended for the common good, adequately made public and derives its legitimacy from the people themselves. The next feature of Igbo positive law that shall be examined is the conformity of Igbo positive laws with *Omenana* - established customs.

The Igbo Positive Law must conform with the Igbo Custom (*Omenana*)

The "ritual ratification" of any major law enacted by the *Oha* is a very significant part of the law making process. Two main features of the ritual ratification are noteworthy. They are:

1. The use of the *Ofo*
2. The special formula of the ratification rite

Now, it is in the use of the *Ọfọ* and the recitation of a special formula that the significance of the "ritual ratification lies". As we examine each of the above separately, it will be seen clearly why an Igbo positive law must not be contrary to the *Omenala*. The reader's attention is drawn to the fact that *Omenala* or *Omenani* is an Igbo word very loosely used to cover the Igbo laws and customs, tradition, etiquette, religion and morality. Mbonu Ojike calls the Igbo natural religion, *"Omenana"*[5]. O'Donnell observed that in Igbo language, "there is no special word for religion"[6]. This observation must not be oversighted.

Mention has already been made of the material form of the *Ọfọ* and its spiritual significance. Njaka summarised it all in the following passage:

> The *Ọfọ* is the central symbol of the Igbo religion. In addition to being a staff of authority, it is an emblem symbolising the links between *Chukwu* and man, the dead and the living, the living and the unborn. The *Ọfọ* also symbolises justice, righteousness, and truth. For these reasons, it plays many important roles in the social, political and the religious life of the Igbo. Hence no serious rite or ceremony can be performed without the *Ọfọ* For example, titles are conferred with the *Ọfọ* . Laws are ratified and consecrated with the *Ọfọ* and none is valid without its being used.[7]

To ratify a law in the Igbo traditional context is to declare that the law is in consonance with the "constitution of the land" and with the custom, religion and morality of the people, in other words with the *Omenana*. To ratify a law on the *Ọfọ* is to confirm that the law so ratified is founded on justice, equity and truth. Above all, a law so consecrated with the *Ọfọ* carries a supernatural sanction besides.

In the ratification rites which usually follows immediately after the *Oha*, the general assembly has approved the law, the following formula is invoked:

> This *iwu* (law) is in accordance with our custom and must be obeyed and respected. Those who refuse to obey the law, may *Ọfọ* kill them.[8]

Ritually, each time the *Ọfọ* is struck on the ground (usually four times, the assembly assent *"ise"* or *"iha"* meaning "let it be so". It is obvious that if

---

[5] Cf Mbonu, O., *op. cit.*, pp. 154-155.

[6] O'Donnell, W., *Religion and Morality among the Igbo of Southern Nigeria*, London, 1931, p. 57.

[7] Njaka, E.N., *op. cit.*, p. 35.

[8] Uchendu, V.C., *op. cit.*, p. 42.

the law is not in keeping with the *Omenana*, it would not be ratified in the first place. And if a law is not so ratified, its validity is to that extent questionable in the eyes of the traditional Igbo.

One may be inclined to ask why in the first instance must an Igbo positive law be in consonance with the *Omenana*? *Omenana* or *Omenala* is the sum total of Igbo religion, morality, custom and etiquette. It is the culmination of the different values - religious, moral, social, political and ethical, which the Igbo cherish and nourish. *Omenana* is therefore the basic foundation on which any new values or innovations must be laid. *Omenana ipso facto* remains a point of reference and a guide against deviation.

Omenana as a distillation of Igbo morality, ensures that any Igbo positive law is in keeping with it or a least not contrary to it. This is why it is absolutely necessary that any piece of legislation must be weighed and balanced on the scale of *Omenana* and if found wanting is thrown over board. And, of course, Igbo morality admits of no relativity. Nor has it any room for situation ethics. Thus, this conformity of the Igbo positive laws with the *Omenana* is a safeguard against the enactment of immoral laws. In the Igbo jurisprudence, therefore, morality and law are inseparable.

Igbo positive laws must not be contrary to the *Omenana* for religious reasons as well. *Omenana* also includes the religion of the people, their beliefs and aspirations. In the previous chapter, we emphasized that the Igbo live in two worlds; the human world and the spirit world. Each is as real to the Igbo as the other. There is a constant interaction between members of both worlds of the Igbo. The ancestors belong to the spirit world but they have direct contact with and influence on the human world. *Omenana*, as customs of the people, is the sum total of the traditions handed down by the ancestors from generation to generation. To go contrary to the *Omenana* is to incur the displeasure of the ancestors. To flout the precepts laid down by the ancestors has far reaching consequences. This is one other reason why a piece of Igbo legislation must not be contrary to the *Omenana*. In other words, as Njaka puts it:

> Law and order are maintained because the ancestors so desire and *Oha* so commands. And the ancestors desire law and order because *Chukwu* must have approved them.

And the only way to ensure that a law is as desired by the ancestors and therefore ultimately in keeping with *Chukwu's* will is by seeing to it that it

---

9 Njaka, E.N., *op. cit.*, p. 46.

does not contradict the *Omenana* which is also the religion of the Igbo as
handed down by the ancestors.

It will be recalled that one of the major causes of the bloody riots of
1929 - 30, which took place at Aba, a highly populated Igbo town, was the
imposition by the British government on the Igbo the system of indirect
rule adopted without reference to the Igbo *Omenana*. The most resentful
aspect of the indirect rule system was the appointment of Warrant Chiefs by
the British Administration. The warrant chiefs "were individuals chosen by
the British with no particular reference to their position in the native
society.[10]

The arbitrary appointment of Warrant Chiefs was not in accordance
with the Igbo *Omenana* especially since the people who were selected for
the post were "those who impressed the District Commissioner with their
courage to come forward and meet the Europeans. The traditional rulers
seldom passed this test, and so were, for the most part, left out.[11] For men
of dubious characters in the persons of the Warrant Chiefs to be entrusted
with the administration of justice in Igboland was clearly contrary to the
Igbo *Omenana*.

The Warrant Chiefs were backed by the coercive force of the British
Administration. But the Igbo could not be intimidated for too long. In
1929, Okugo, a Warrant Chief from Oloko touched off a massive protest of
Igbo women when he attempted to assess their property in his area.

The people's grievance welled up to a point where they could no longer
contain them. Soon afterwards, the Aba riots ensued.

....in which feeling against taxation and against the Warrant chiefs,
together with discontent at the low price of palm oil, flared into serious
disturbance and bloodshed. And there can be no doubt that beneath the overt
grievances lay a deep unconscious, cultural protest.[12]

Indeed the riot was a conscious cultural protest: a protest against the blatant
violation of the Igbo *Omenana*, the "sacred" law and custom of the land.

I have cited the Aba riot which took place in recent past to show that
the Igbo do not take kindly to any system, law or innovation which violate
the *Omenana*. And the reasons why the *Omenana* must not be sacrificed on
the altar of innovation or modernization have been clearly stated too.

---

[10] Green, M.M., *op. cit.*, p. 4.

[11] Nwabueze, B.O., *The Mechinery of Justice in Nigeria*, London, Butterworth &
Co (Publishers) Ltd, 1963. p. 70

[12] Green, MM., *op. cit.*, p. 4.

It stands clear from our analysis of the five essential elements of the Igbo positive laws that any valid positive law must be legitimate, reasonable, sufficiently promulgated, intended for the common good and must not be found contrary to the *Omenana*, the established Igbo custom. Having seen the main characteristic features of Igbo positive laws, we may now proceed to discuss the ends of laws in Igbo traditional society.

The End of Laws in the Igbo Traditional Society

Law, in the traditional Igbo society is always and in all cases a means to an end. Laws in general are means of achieving certain ends in the native society and not the ends per se. What are these ends which the Igbo laws purport to achieve? These are what we have set out to set down in this section.

Already, note has been taken of the two main divisions of Igbo laws - the human and divine laws. While the ends of both laws ultimately converge at a point, the former differ from the latter in its immediate goal. The end of the Igbo positive laws is social harmony while that of the divine law is spiritual harmony. The human laws relate to the immediate social needs and aspiration whereas the divine laws seek to guide man in his relationship with *Chukwu*, other spirits and the ancestor so that he will ultimately secure a place in the spirit world, the happy abode of the ancestors.

Igbo human laws are social instruments by which diverse and often conflicting interests of the members of the society are regulated in such a way that common interest of the community as a whole is placed above individual interests. The laws are further the means by which the rights of the individuals in the Igbo society are secured and protected. Now, when the various interests of the members of the society have been so tailored as to be in line with the overall interests of the society by means of law and when the rights of the individuals are at the same time guaranteed by the laws, a peaceful and harmonious society necessarily emerges.

As the Igbo exercise due legislative care to ensure that their laws are just, fair and honest and since justice, fairness and honesty are vital and indispensable elements in the making of a peaceful and harmonious society, the Igbo human laws are best equipped to achieve this end. Besides, the main features of Igbo human laws which we have already examined are positive features which make for an egalitarian society.

Man's social, economic and political ends are not absolute so are the laws by means of which these ends are reached. Because the ends of Igbo positive laws are not absolute, they are subject to amendment or total abrogation. If a known Igbo law is no longer serving as means of achieving social harmony and peace, that law loses its validity and must be either amended or entirely revoked. Even the customary laws are subject to amendment in the interest of social harmony and peace so long as such laws concern the people in their social milieu.

Green's observation is quite correct. She writes:

> Parliament in the Middle Ages in England may, according to some historians, have been a law-declaring rather than a law making body, but an Igbo community, far from resting on immemorial custom, seems always ready for new departures even to the extent of discussing, as Owerri was doing, the alteration of such apparently fundamental conditions as rules governing exogamy.[13]

In short, any Igbo human law remains effective as long as it is an instrument of peace and social harmony. And the ultimate end of Igbo positive laws is to build a harmonious society in which alone progress and prosperity could thrive.

On the other hand, the divine laws, the breach of which is an abomination, have spiritual harmony as their ultimate end. The Igbo live simultaneously in two worlds - the human and spirit worlds. A typical Igbo strives not to dissociate himself from the spiritual community by violating the taboos or by involvement in any *nso* behaviour. In other words he endeavours to keep the divine laws.

By keeping the divine laws, the Igbo live in spiritual union with the ancestors, the spirits and ultimately with *Chukwu*. At the end of his sojourn in the human world, the Igbo hope for a place in the spirit world, the abode of the ancestors, only if they have lived a clean life by not violating the divine laws, by being untainted by any *nso* or *alu* behaviour or breach of any taboo.

Now, the violation of the divine laws, all *nso* or *alu* behaviour are said to be a pollution of the land, *imeru ala*. One *nso* behaviour pollutes the entire land and temporarily the spiritual communion with the ancestors are suspended because of the abomination. To restore the spiritual harmony with the ancestors, a ritual purification is needed. Otherwise, the entire community may share in the punishment the ancestors may send. Thus, there is need to maintain the spiritual harmony with the members of the spirit world especially the ancestors and other friendly spirits. The end of the divine laws is to ensure that this spiritual harmony is maintained at individual and community levels. The individuals who have maintained this

---

[13] Green, MM., *op. cit.*, p. 132.

spiritual harmony by not violating the divine laws would have lived an untarnished social life and, consequently, be welcomed in the spirit land of the ancestors when they die.

The end of the divine laws is spiritual and absolute. It is absolute in the sense that they are supposed to regulate men's behaviour so that they can achieve their ultimate spiritual goal which is having a place in the spirit world, the happy abode of the ancestors. Unlike the Igbo human laws, the divine laws are not subject to amendment.

The Igbo human laws and the divine laws, although having different ultimate ends, are nevertheless all useful and effective in curbing men's excesses in the society. They are both indispensable in fostering justice, fairness, honesty and equality among the members of the society. Both laws enhance social harmony directly or indirectly.

Chapter 5

The Igbo Positive Laws And Their Native Religion

The Igbo native religion which embodies their morality and custom occupies a central position in the field of Igbo human laws. In direct opposition to the spirit and tenet of legal positivism, the Igbo jurisprudence does not admit any separation of legality from morality. The principles of *Ofoism* is invoked not only in the making of the laws, nor only in the keeping of the same but also in the actual breach of the laws. To substantiate the above assertion, I shall discuss the following points: Law making, Maintenance of law; and Law in breach as they occur in the Igbo society.

Law Making

Already the technical procedure of law making in the Igbo native society has been discussed. Here we are specifically concerned with the religious aspect of law making.

The second but a very important stage in the legislative process is the "ritual ratification" of the law so made. The two essential features of the "ritual ratification" of any law are the use of *Ofo* and the ritual formula itself. We have noted earlier on the symbolic representation of the *Ofo* And we may recall its religious significance here:

> The *Ofo* is the central symbol of the Igbo religion. In addition to being a staff of authority, it is an emblem symbolizing the links between *Chukwu* and man, the dead and the living, the living and the unborn. The *Ofo* also symbolizes justice, righteousness, and truth. For these reason, it plays many important roles in the social, political, and religious life of the Igbo. Hence no serious rite or ceremony can be performed without the *Ofo* . For example, titles are conferred with the *Ofo* . Laws are ratified and consecrated with *Ofo* and none is valid without its being used.[1]

The ratification ritual is performed exclusively by the *Ofo* holders who are men of integrity and are believed to have the closest links with the ancestors. The following formula is usually employed:

> This *iwu* - Law is in accordance with our custom and must be obeyed and respected. Those who refuse to obey the law, may *Ofo* kill them.

---

[1] Njaka, E.N., *Igbo Political Culture*, Ibid p. 35.

Each time the *Ọfọ* is struck on the ground, the assembly assents with *ise* or *iha*, meaning "let it be so".This done, the law is regarded as (ratified) and consecrated and may now be promulgated.

The ritual ratification has a religious and moral import. By consecrating the law of the land on the *Ọfọ* , the law acquires a new dimension - a supernatural one.

For since the *Ọfọ* is an emblem symbolizing the links between *Chukwu*, God, and man the ritual ratification of the law on the *Ọfọ* elevates it from human to supernatural level and thus raises it from the mundane to the sublime. The consequence of this consecration is that whoever breaks this law stands condemned not only by the human society but also by the supernatural.

As one of the *Ọfọ* holders declares that the *Iwu* - the law in question is in accordance with the custom of the land and must be obeyed and respected and wishing in the name of the assembly that those who refuse to obey the law be killed by the *Ọfọ* , the assembly assents in unison - *ise* or *iha* (may it be so). This unanimous assent is significant. It meant that everyone has freely agreed that any offender would incur the displeasure of the supernatural besides the stipulated social sanctions.

For the breach of the law to incur the wrath of the supernatural, such law must be morally right, and just. Thus, any law that must be ratified on the *Ọfọ* must be seen to conform with the moral code and ethical values of *Ọfọism*. This will be further dealt with in a different section of this chapter.

Meanwhile, the place of religion right in the making of the law in a typical Igbo society has been shown. The native religion is to this extent a recognized instrument in the process of law making in the Igbo native set-up.

Maintenance of the Law

In general, the Igbo do not have   permanent law enforcement agents of western style, although an ad hoc group could be appointed to perform that function, if need be. But the fact is that the native Igbo keeps the laws of the land not merely for fear of being caught by the law enforcement agent but mainly because the principles and doctrines of his religion require him to do so. In Njaka's words:

Law and order are maintained because the ancestors so desire and oha so commands. And the ancestors desire law and order because *Chukwu* must have approved them.[2]

The "*Odibendi*" concept of *Ofoism* generates an internal religious motion which drives the *Ofoists* to keep the laws not only those of his homeland but those of other land and clime he may find himself in. In this context, "*Odibendi*" means the institutions - legal, social, religious, etc. which characterize any given community and are acknowledged by the members of that community.

The belief in *Odibendi*, that is, the concept that the institutions of a people must be respected leads the native Igbo to obey the laws of the land as though he is fulfilling his religious obligation by so doing. Guided by this belief, he obeys the laws out of conviction rather than for fear of some external punishment. A people that have been so taught by their religion to obey the laws and to respect other people's institutions do not need any standing coercive force.

Furthermore, the laws are obeyed because the ancestors so desire. Already, we have noted the role of the ancestors in the social and political life of the Igbo. In general, the Igbo strives to lead a good life so that he might be made welcome by the ancestors when he dies. Since the ancestors wish that peace and harmony should reign in their families, and law and order make for peace and harmony, they desire that any law, which is not contrary to the tradition that they handed down, must be obeyed.

The consequences of going against the wishes and institutions of the ancestors are far reaching. As Green pointed out:

> Perhaps one of the most interesting ways in which social disruption is prevented is in the beliefs current in this society about the causes of death and disaster.[3]

The Igbo who flouts the law of the land consecrated on the *Ofo* and thus approved by the ancestors may be punished either directly or indirectly depending on the nature of the law so broken. Ill-fortune, sickness or death could be the result of his action. A more dreadful punishment would be the non accessibility to the spirit land - the longed for happy abode of the ancestors. Here, again, we discover another religious motivation for keeping the law in Igbo native society.

---

2 Njaka, E.N. *op. cit.*, p. 46.
3 Green, M.M., op. cit., p. 94.

In the absence of any standing law enforcement agents as a recognised institution, the Igbo native religion by means of its doctrines, principles and ethics prevent the breaking of law and order in the community. Laws are therefore obeyed out of religious convictions rather than out of legal pressure. And finally, the fear of the supernatural rather than the fear of man is the main deterrent to prospective law-breakers.

Having seen the role of the Igbo native religion in the making and keeping of the law we shall now proceed to examine the place of the religion in the adjudication of (legal disputes) cases.

Law in Breach

In no other sphere of Igbo legal life does the religion play such a decisive role than in the adjudication of cases. The Igbo employs his religion in settling legal disputes, in determining whose cause is just in a given case and in the punishment of the offender whether known or unknown.

In the event of any breach of the law, the injured person has a number of legitimate actions to choose from. If the offence is not grave, the injured party may refer the matter to his kinsmen - *umunna* if the accused is of the same *umunna*. Otherwise, the case could be resolved by the village-elders or any of the judicial institutions discussed in the previous chapter. If the offence is of grave nature, a supernatural tribunal is expected to adjudicate. I shall first describe a typical Igbo "assizes" with a view to highlighting its religious phase before discussing the supernatural tribunals and how they work.

A judicial assembly, be it that of the elders, kinsmen, age-group or the village, if it is to command credibility must open deliberations on a religious note. Usually, the plaintiff and the accused are committed to say the truth and the arbitrators to stand for the just cause in a ritual ceremony performed even before the litigants begin stating their cases for hearing.

Green, in her book, *Ibo Village Affairs* described the ritual ceremony with which a typical Igbo judicial assembly opened its session. Her account may well be cited here for its objectivity and authenticity: "The two litigants were then told to bring palm wine for them. Each produced a gourd full, G. buying hers with 1d provided by one of her kinsmen. Those present drank, so far as I remember. Then N.O. the senior man, took a cup of palm wine and poured it on the four *Ọfọ*, saying as he did so:

Onye o wu, ya wuru ya.
Onye o wuhu, ya awula ya.

Literarily:
"Whoever it is, let it be him,

Whoever it is not, let it not be him".

That is, whoever is guilty, let him be guilty: whoever is not guilty, let him not be guilty.

The second most senior man of village, Nwa Onye Okoro head of the big extended family of Umu Nwa Ebodim, took a small chick brought by the defendant, and holding it up, pulled its head off and let the blood drip on the *Ofo*, and then threw it away. It would not be eaten by anyone. Having done this, the same man who had killed the chick spoke as follows:

Onye huru ezi okwu n'uka a, na-ekwuhu,Ofo gbuo ya, Ha!

Onye nuru ezi okwu n'uka a, na ekwuhu,Ofo gbuo ya, Ha!

Onye na-agaghi ekpe nkanne,Ofo gbuo ya, Ha!

That is:
"whoever sees the truth in this case, and does not say it, may *Ofo* kill him, ha! Whoever speaks a lie, may *Ofo* kill him, ha! Whoever hears a word in this case and does not speak it, may *Ofo* kill him, ha! Whoever does not judge a-right, may *Ofo* kill him, ha!"

All present joined, as is customary, in the Ha! at the end of each phrase. As they did so the *Ofo* holders who, with other people were crouching round their *Ofo*, picked them up and knocked them on the ground and everyone else present either knocked their hands on the ground, or, with the same intention, on their sides. Any swearing by *Ofo* seems to be accompanied by this cry of "Ha!" which, on its falling tone, sounds almost like a snarl, and certainly gives the impression of a curse. After this rite people sat down again and the defendant began to state his case."[4]

Any typical Igbo judicial assembly would follow the opening rite described above by Green. It must be noted that the essential feature of this opening ceremony is the invocation of the supernatural to oversee the goings on. The opening ceremony may at times be informal but the use of *Ofo* may not be omitted. Here again, Green's remarks is quite apt:

> In considering procedure it is worth noticing that the ritual with *Ofo* was of no small importance. It has, of course, the effect of introducing a supernatural sanction, a feature with which all who have any experience of Ibo judicial methods are familiar in principle.[5]

---

[4] Green, M.M. *op. cit.* pp. 120-121.

[5] Green, M.M. *op. cit.* p. 121.

It is apparent that even when a purely human arbitration is called for in a legal dispute, the supernatural must not be left out entirely. This is why the judicial procedure adumbrated above opened on a religious note.

Disputes could also be resolved by a direct appeal to the supernatural for adjudication. This may take the form of swearing or consulting the oracle. The supreme court of the land are the supernatural tribunes and their verdict is final. Thus, when swearing is resorted to as a judicial method, no further action is expected to be taken by either parties. The same applies to oracular verdicts.

As a legitimate legal action, the injured party may ask the accused to swear on a tutelar deity of his choice to prove his innocence. The course of action is usually taken in a protracted case where the intricacies of the matter make it difficult to discern who is right or wrong in the case.

On the other hand, the accused may opt to swear on any powerful "*Alusi*" in order to free himself from the accusation. If the plaintiff accepts the accused's offer to swear, he is bound to regard the dispute as closed and to await for the supernatural judgment. The grave consequences of swearing falsely have been well orchestrated earlier on. It is pointless repeating them here but suffice it to say that the perjurer may die as the result or he may suffer grave misfortune or illness. The more dreadful consequence is that the perjurer's family and sometimes, the entire village may suffer from some obscure illness which may put the lineage in danger of complete extinction.

Swearing as a legitimate judicial method and which in the belief of the native Igbo is the one of the assured ways of obtaining absolute justice (the other method being consultation of the oracle), has survived western influences. This further illustrates the fundamentality of this judicial method in the Igbo judicial system.

The British colonial administrators fully aware of the relative value of swearing in the native judicial system and capitalizing on the religious beliefs of the people that make this judicial method effective, encouraged the practice. Thus, in the Native Courts set up by the British colonial administration, the plaintiffs are made to swear on the *Ofo* or *Ikenga* or other recognised traditional religious objects before presenting their cases to the judges. This practice has survived till date.

The traditional Igbo have guarded this judicial method jealously. The early missionaries who first came to Igboland underestimating the value and the importance of this judicial method, described it as "paganish" and set out to abolish it or at least to stop the converts from taking to that kind of supernatural adjudication. This was one of the sources of conflict between the *Ofoists* and the early christian converts.

Even in the recent past, the *Ofoists* have insisted that in all situations and cases where the use of swearing is recommended as a necessary judicial course of action, no member of the community may abstain from conforming without facing grave consequences. But the christian converts who have grown in population have damned these consequences and after a series of conflicts between the *Ofoists* and the church members, a compromise has been reached.

It happened in my own village and I was also an eye-witness. A young man had died and as usual, he was thought to have died of poisoning. All his close friends especially those who were his partners in trade were summoned to swear on the village powerful deity to prove that they are innocent of the blood of the deceased young man. All agreed to swear for this was the only way they could extricate themselves from the ugly accusation. But the christians among them made it clear that they would not swear on the said deity but on a Bible. After a violent protest by the natives, they at last conceded.

On the appointed day, the priest of the local deity came and led the *Ofoists* in the swearing ritual. After all have sworn according to the *Ofoistic* prescription, the Roman Catholic priest who was invited by the christians presented the Bible on which they swore using the same words as their non-christian counterparts. With this new development in the Igbo country, swearing, whether on the *Ofo* or on *Alusi* or on the Bible, is now widely recognised all over Igboland as a legitimate judicial method accessible to all, *Ofoists* and non-*Ofoists*.

I have mentioned in passing that the supernatural is the final arbiter, "the last court of appeal", in modern parlance, with regard to disputes within and without the precinct of law. In a recent land dispute between the people of Abagana and the people of Umunachi, two neighbouring village-groups, the traditional head of Umunachi, Chief F.E.O. Onochie, offered to swear to an oath that the land in dispute belonged to his people.[6]

The Chief made this proposal as the last move in the Igbo judicial process. He wanted to appeal to the supernatural to be the final Arbiter and to vindicate the cause of his people. The traditional head of the other party in dispute refused. If Chief F.E.O. Onochie, the traditional head of Umanachi people, had been allowed to swear to an oath the opposing party would have been obliged to relinquish the disputed piece of land in-toto and the matter would have been declared *res judicata*.

---

6 Cf. Public notice: Abagana-Umunachi Land dispute. *Weekly Star*, p. 12, Sunday, Nov. 8, 1981.

The fact that as recent as 1981, the use of swearing as judicial method is advocated by even men who have acquired a measure of western education and training is a clear indication that the Igbo native religion with its doctrines and creeds, still exert a considerable influence on the Igbo legal and judicial systems. It further shows that a recourse to the supernatural in the form of swearing is the final legal or judicial action opened to an injured party.

Oracular verdict, which is also regarded as final in any given case or situation, being itself supernatural in nature, is highly respected and acceptable by the Igbo, both in the past and in the present. It is therefore proper at this juncture to recount the episode that took place at Ogbunike, a historic Igbo town. The story that follows was published in one of Nigeria's Newspapers, *Weekly Star* The story went as follows:

Some henchmen of the deposed Igwe of Ogbunike, Chief Umenyiora, reportedly consulted seven oracles at the Ogbunike Town Hall on October 23, 1981 and got the shock of their lives.

The oracle told them that all the Ogbunike people who invoked jujus and employed masquerades to ostracise and intimidate members and supporters of NPP in the area will now face the wrath of the very gods they invoked.

The doomed persons (including some *ndichie and umuada* daughters of the land) had resorted to invoking the jujus and letting loose, masquerades on NPP supporters and ostracising them in order to intimidate them into joining the NPN.

The consultation of the oracles on Thursday, October 23, 1981, followed a series of mishaps which had befallen certain elements in the town in recent months.

These tragic events were climaxed by the deposition of Chief John Umenyiora as the Igwe of Ogbunike following a judicial commission of inquiry which found him to have been the mastermind behind the invocation of the jujus and the use of masquerades.

The seven oracles consulted on October 23, 1981 were reportedly unanimous in their verdict that the wrath of the gods they invoked against innocent citizens of the town is now visiting those who invoked them.

Those henchmen including some *ndichie*, and *umuada* had brought seven powerful native doctors to the town hall on October 23, 1981 to consult their oracles about the cause of the tragedies and the solution to the problem.

Three of the native doctors were from Ogbunike while four were from other towns. The first oracle said that the ndichie committed gross abomination which filled the town with darkness. This oracle said that the gods are so angry that more calamity was looming over the town. The native doctor therefore packed his oracle and went away saying he did not want to involve himself in the nemesis that was closing in on the town.

The second oracle identified the darkness covering the town with the anger of eight gods particularly the *Ogba* or god of Ogbunike cave and the dreadful *Iyi-Oji* juju of Nkwelle-Ezunaka. According to this oracle, the *ndichie* had smeared the land with abomination and infamy. The *Ogba* was therefore very angry with them and immediate appeasement was necessary.

The third oracle said that the *ndichie* and their mentors brought false accusations against innocent citizens of the town. In their effort to destroy and eliminate these innocent citizens, the oracle said, they committed gross abomination against the land. This oracle said that none of the people accused of having an eye on the traditional throne of Ogbunike was interested in the chieftaincy. It said that they (the accusers) were guilty not only of gross abomination but also of lies, deceit and setting confusion in the town.

The oracle said that those who had invoked jujus against innocent citizens must immediately revoke those jujus and purge themselves of all the abominations they had committed to avert the boomerang now descending on them, as well as those who had followed their directives in ignorance.

The oracle said that the *ndichie* committed gross abomination by declaring sanction against innocent people and ostracising even women and using masquerades to announce the names of women ostracised. It said that it is an abomination for masquerades to call the names of women.

The remaining oracles confirmed the verdict of the preceding ones and said that the *ndichie* and others who participated in the invocation of jujus and ostracising innocent people were being haunted by the shadows of their iniquities. Disappointed by the unanimous verdict of the oracles, and afraid of the heavy hand of nemesis closing in on them, the *ndichie* were said to have frantically procured a goat, a fowl, four yams, kolanuts and palm wine for immediate appeasement of *Ogba*.

But there was controversy about where the sacrifice was to be offered. One of the local native doctors said the sacrifice would be offered at *Ogba* shrine. But the *ndichie* who were afraid that that process would deprive them of the meat and other convivialities from the juju feast, insisted that the sacrifice would be offered in a little cemented hole in front of the town hall and which, legend said, burst into the cave.

They then grabbed the goat and fowl, slaughtered them, poured the blood into the hole, smeared the cement around the hole with the blood, and made a juju feast with the meat.[7]

Oracular verdicts as we have seen in the case narrated above are final and are generally taken seriously. The *ndichie* of Ogbunike consulted the oracles to find out the cause of the mishaps that had befallen certain members of their community. The oracle declared that the *ndichie* and their accomplice are pursuing unjust cause by victimizing innocent citizens. They were warned of impending doom unless they retraced their steps and appeased the god of Ogbunike, otherwise known an *Ogba*.

In obedience to the oracular verdict, the *ndichie* had to repent and offered sacrifice to appease the god. In this way, a protracted dispute between the supporters of NPP and NPN, two opposing political parties, which had led to a periodic upsurge of violence in the town was brought under control.

The Ogbunike episode which took place as recent as 1981, clearly indicates that even in the present day Igbo society, whenever law and order are threatened as a result of violent dispute between individuals or groups, and when the law of the land alone could not secure the life and property of the people, only an appeal to the supernatural could restore peace and order and create a social atmosphere in which no one may feel a sense of injustice.

Emerging from the foregoing is the fact that the Igbo positive laws, effective as they are in promoting peace and order and in protecting the basic rights of the members of the community, nevertheless, need the unction of the native religion to make them all the more effective in their essential role.

For the religion has been seen to have a place in the making of the laws themselves. By means of its doctrines and principles, the religion prepares the minds of the people to obey the laws. In this way, it is instrumental in the maintenance of the laws. In the event of the breach of the laws, the native religion provides judicial forum through which the injured party may seek justice and redress.

Indeed, the Igbo operate a political and legal system in which their native religion occupies a central position. It is a system that operates in such a way that the spiritual and material needs of members of the community are simultaneously emphasized and equally catered for. It is however, a system with a bleak future as its survival depends largely on the survival of the native religion that makes it workable.

---

[7] Cf. "Greatest Shock in Ogbunike", *Weekly Star*, Sunday, Nov., 1981, p. 1.

Chapter 6

The Notion and Exercise Of Rights In The Igbo Traditional Society

Law connotes right and it is proper to examine the notion and exercise of rights in Igbo country having discussed extensively the nature of laws in the native Igbo community. Sources of individual rights have been subjects of feverish dispute and endless controversy.[+]

The Igbo notion of right can only be understood with reference to concrete social realities. For the Igbo rights are not simply abstract concepts outlined in a constitutional preamble but concrete social phenomena understood and exercised by all and sundry. Thus the notion of right must be examined in the context and light of social justice. It is in fact, from the taproots of social justice that individual rights in Igbo traditional setting draws nurture and strength.

And social justice demands mutual and reciprocal respect of rights and interests.

Individual rights are highly respected in Igbo country. The basic rights and the ones that are held as natural and sacred are the right to life and property. That these rights are natural, inalienable and fundamental in Igbo society is evident from:-

(1)	The grave consequence that will follow any interference with an individual right to any of the above.
(2)	Interference with another person's right to life is regarded as direct assault to *Ala*, the earth goddess believed to be the source of life.
(3)	Interference with one's property is an indirect interference with his life. We shall examine each of the above points further.

The right to life is held as natural and sacred by the Igbo and any interference with it in any form has grave consequences. For this reason, homicide is regarded by the Igbo as the most horrible crime. A man who commits homicide ceases to be a member of the society and is stripped of

---

[+] Cf. Right and law in Thomas Hobbess Ethical and Political theory, (A Master's thesis submitted by me), Urban University Rome, 1980, pp. 2 - 4.

all his civic rights. For each act of murder threatens and undermines the very existence of the society as a corporate body.

The only right reserved for a murderer is the right to die. The murderer must hang himself for his very existence in the Igbo society is no longer recognised. If the murderer runs away, the death penalty awaits him wherever he may be. And since no murderer would be welcome or sympathised with in any Igbo state, he is, as it were, disowned by all human communities he is familiar with. Dying, therefore, the murderer must die.

The gravity of homicide is not mitigated by the circumstance and nature of the crime. However, accidental homicide, though grave, is seen from a different social perspective. Apart from accidental ones homicide whether as a result of direct violence to the victim or through occult means such as secret poisoning, magic, sorcery or witchcraft is subject to the same sanctions and penalty. The Igbo regard this right to life so fundamental and so inalienable that no person or institution has the authority or power to order the execution of a murderer.

"It is important to realise that the village has no power to impose capital punishment. Infact, no social group or institution has this power. Every thing affecting the life of the villager is regulated by custom. The life of the individual is highly respected. It is protected by the earth goddess. The villagers can bring social pressure, but the murderer must hang himself".[1]

The above observation made by the anthropologist Uchendu further demonstrates the inalienability and fundamentality of the right to life and the sanctity of the human person as a whole.

We have been discussing the social consequences that attend any interference with the individual's right to life in Igbo traditional society, consequences grave enough to match the cause which set them in motion.

The right to life is considered sacred and inalienable because it is a right conferred on everybody by *Ala*-the earth goddess and protected by her. Homicide is therefore an offence against *Ala*, the earth deity. And we have already noted in the previous chapter that any offence against *Ala*, the constitutional deity is an abomination- *Alu. Ala* will not let that offence go unpunished. The Igbo regard such an offence as a "pollution of the Land". It is a breach of the natural law and an interference with the natural right of the individual. The point I am making here is that whatever the Igbo associates with *Ala* must be regarded as sacred, fundamental and must be respected as such. The life of the individual, is one of such things and the right to it is

---

[1] Uchendu V.C., *op. cit.*, pp. 42-43.

natural and sacred and the Igbo hold it as such. Thus, even when homicide is accidental, the culprit, is suspended from his membership of the community. His interdiction remains in force until the cleansing ceremony called *Ikpu aru* has been performed. This is then followed by a special kind of feast called *Oriko* or *Nligbo* and the person is again a responsible Igbo citizen with all his civic rights restored in-toto.

Since the right to life is natural and inalienable as it is conferred on the individual by *Ala* - the mother earth, believed by the Igbo to be the source of all life, no individual should interfere with his own life. The Igbo society therefore condemns suicide as illicit and disowns the man who kills himself. If a man commits suicide, he has brought a big shame on the members of his *Umunna* - family. Nobody is expected to mourn for him. He is denied a "good" burial ceremony which is given only to persons who have lived untarnished social life according to the principles of *Ofoism*. Because, the Igbo regard the right to life as natural and inalienable and because this is a God-given right, abortion is extremely intolerable in Igbo traditional society. There is though no specific sanction imposed for an act of abortion but a woman who commits abortion falls in status and reputation among the women folk. By the same token, a man who is known to be a habitual accomplice in abortion acts loses face with his menfolk and may never be called upon to hold any religious office or lead any ritual ceremony.

It emerges clear from the foregoing that the Igbo hold the right to life as natural and inalienable and by means of social and religious sanctions, any form of interference with it is prevented or at least discouraged.

The right to property is highly respected in Igbo country and like the right to life it is held as natural, fundamental and inalienable. And the right to property is expressed by the Igbo in terms of social justice. This idea is clearly expressed in some popular Igbo names among which are the following: "*Okemefuna*" which can be rendered as "let me not lose my rightful share". This name portrays the Igbo sense of distributive justice. "Okemuo" means literally "share from God". It expresses the same notion as "Okechi" another popular Igbo name meaning "share from God". Both understood in the light of social justice express the Igbo social reality that the "share" or the 'right' given to the individual by God cannot be taken away from him, in other words it is inalienable. The concept of God as a distributor or sharer of social goods is expressed by the Igbo name "Chijioke" meaning it is God who distributes. We have to note here that *Oke* to which other words can be prefixed is an Igbo word which could mean "share" or "right" depending on the context in which the word is used. "*Oke*" of course implies a material good and a right to it thereof. Thus, in

Igbo social context, it is the right to one's material goods or property and the right to acquire them by fair and just means that generated the strong sense of social justice as we shall see later in this chapter.

With regard to the right to property, any interference with it in any way whatsoever stands condemned by the Igbo society. This is why stealing is a grave offence and a classical sinner is a thief. If one looked at his neighbour as though his neighbour wronged him, his neighbour's reaction will be to ask him with an air of innocence *"EZULUM IFE GI?* (did I steal your property?). This again shows how much value and importance the Igbo place on individual's private property and the right to hold and maintain it without interference. The following statement taken from Green's anthropological report on the Igbo people is relevant here. It reads:

> The attitude of Igbo to property is again emphasised by (the) elaborate means of discouraging all accessories to the act of stealing....[2]

The treatment of a thief vary in accordance with the nature of the things stolen. If the thief is caught in the very act of stealing, he is beaten up mercilessly and taken round the market place with the stolen property tied around him. He is jeered and mocked at by passers-by. Nobody sympathises with a thief. There is infact a saying in Igbo that "a thief is nobody's brother" - (*onye ori aburo nwanne madu*) A thief has no social regard and has no say either among members of his age-grade or in the community at large.

Stealing of seedlings and other kinds of theft like removing a property on which a sample of earth is placed to indicate ownership are regarded as *Aru* or *Nso-Ala* (Abomination).[3] This kind of theft, though infringement on or interference with the other people's right to property as other kinds of theft, is regarded as specially a fundamental breach of the law. The background of the Igbo attitude to this particular kind of theft needs to be further elaborated.

Farming is the mainstay of Igbo economy. It is infact the major source revenue to the individuals and the society at large and provide the bulk of the population with the most subsistent needs. In short it is the major means of livelihood in the native society before the recent growth of market oriented economy which ushered in an era of "business-economy" in Igbo land. Seedlings are therefore very vital property to the Igbo for without it, reproduction or propagation will be impossible as there will be ultimately nothing to plant in the farm. This would ultimately remove one's means of

---

[2] Green, M.M., *op. cit.*, p. 115.
[3] Cf. Njaka E.N. *op. cit.*, p. 41.

livelihood and the attendant horrors of starvation to death. On this score, stealing of seedlings is regarded as a direct interference with the means of one's livelihood and is treated as such. Stealing of yam seedlings is even more grave. This is because yam is a crop around which much of the social and religious life of Igbo centre. The stealing of seedlings and the yam seedling in particular is therefore a taboo.

In general, the Igbo cherish his right to private property. Hence the Igbo name "Nkem-dilim" meaning literally "let my own remain for me". In other words, do not interfere with my property or affairs. And the Igbo pledges not to interfere with others' rights to property. This makes the Igbo to ask, "Ejimkonye? That is to say "am I in possession of what does not belong to me by right? "Ejimkonye" is a popular Igbo name. In order that he be not tempted to interfere with another person's property, the Igbo prays and wishes thus: "Nke akam akonam". This means literally "may I not be in want of personal property". In other words, may I have my own personal belongings (so as not to desire those of others). Expressing contentment in whatever measure of earthly possession he has, the Igbo says "Okechinyelu". This means the much one's *chi* gives him, let him take that much with satisfaction.

This much has to be said about the right to life and property-rights regarded by the Igbo as natural and inalienable. With reference to the Igbo attitude to life and property, based on concrete social phenomena, I have been able to support the view that the rights to life and property are regarded as sacred, natural, fundamental and inalienable by the Igbo.

In the traditional Igbo society, the individual rights to freedom of expression, of thought and action are recognised, respected nd cherished in keeping with the principles of "Ọhacracy". The Igbo in recognition of these rights maintain that, "*Aka di onye mma ka ọna ehi na-isi*". Translated literally, it means, "One supports his head with whichever hand he likes". This is to say that one has the right to think and act freely unimpeded.

"Ọhacracy" the Igbo system of government promotes the rights to freedom of expression, of thought and of action. This freedom is enjoyed by all in public and in private. On the public level, during the meeting of the general assembly called 'Ọha' public matters are thrown open for discussion. Every villager who can contribute to the discussion is given a hearing. No one is denied a hearing during public discussions and all shades of opinion are considered before decision is finally taken. To stop someone from expressing himself in the public gathering or to interrupt his speech suddenly is an offence. The person who so debars another from expressing himself or, who rudely interrupts him in the course of his speech is by that act a target of public obloquy. His action is regarded as detrimental to public order and peace and is treated as such.

The effect of this right to freedom of expression, thought and action is that for any social group to carry out a decision there .nust have been a consensus among the members. Otherwise, a dissenting member is not bound by the decision and is not responsible for the action of the group. There is no form of censorship in Igbo "Ohacracy". Every villager is free to hold any opinion and to express the same in whatever way he can. Provided that his actions do not directly interfere with the rights of others he is free to act and to comport himself in a manner and way he chooses.

Based on the rights to freedom of expression, thought and actions, religious liberty is guaranteed in the Igbo traditional society. *Ofoism*, the Igbo natural religion which largely influences the Igbo people's concepts and way of life is instrumental in guaranteeing religious freedom. The Igbo religion is basically a non-aggressive and non-evangelising religion. Because of its belief in *Odibendi* and *Omumendi*, it does not proselytize. In this context, *odibendi* means the institutions and culture which characterise a state and are respected as long as they serve the state and likewise, *omumendi* affirms that each state has its own customs and way of life as long as people of the state continue to welcome them.

By means of these two concepts, *Ofoism* guarantees each people their own customs and characteristics; it assumes that each town or state has its way of life, and this leads to toleration of the customs and belief of every other people with whom the Igbo come in contact. The Igbo religion accepts the principle that customs differ from one place to another and that customs are good for those who accept them but may not suffice for or serve others. This realisation prepares the *Ofoist* to move into a strange area without disturbing its people. The Igbo religion therefore requires its adherents to respect the rights of others within and without the Igbo states especially the rights to freedom of conscience, thought and expression. I shall further discuss the role of religion in the preservation of individual rights in Igbo society in the next section.

The Roles of Igbo Laws and Religion in the Preservation of Individual Rights

Ideally, to secure the individual rights in the society is the *raison d'etre* of the laws. Every society has an obligation to protect the rights of its members and the society achieves this objective by means of law. Thus, there could be no need for laws if there were no humans rights. Here, laws are to be understood as positive laws or human laws. Before we proceed to examine the roles of Igbo laws and religion in protecting the rights of the individual in the society it would be necessary to know the source from where the Igbo believe that their rights emanate.

Ontological Basis of Rights

The Igbo holds that men are born with certain rights which they regard as inalienable. This concept is expressed practically in their attitude towards certain rights. The Igbo hold that every individual is born with the right to life and the right to the means of preserving it ie, the right to property. These and other rights like the right to freedom of expression etc. accrue to individuals because they are human beings. This concept is opposed to the tenets of the school of thought which holds that whatever right the individuals have are conferred on them by the society and that without society there would cease to be rights.

The Igbo strongly hold that life comes from God. It is the "*Chi*" alone who can interfere with life for it belongs to him. Thus no one has the authority to interfere with another person's life, not even the society for any reason whatsoever. Logically, the right to life comes at birth and the society does but ensure its protection from interference. We shall recall what Uchendu says in this regard.

> Everything affecting the life of the villager is regulated by custom. The life of the individual is highly respected, it is protected by the earth-goddess.[4]

The right to life remains with the individual and is not conferred or determined by the society or any individual or groups of individual.

The right to the means of preserving life is also born with the individual. In realisation of this fact, land which is the most important asset of the Igbo people, (being the source of livelihood of a people who depend on farming for subsistence) is accessible to everybody.

"Land is (therefore) the most important asset to the people. It is a source of security which is emotionally protected from alienation. It is believed that a people cannot have too much land and that no opportunity to acquire rights in land should be lost.[5]

An individual who interrupts another villager during his speech or who stops him from expressing his opinion in a public gathering or any other gathering will be aggressively rebuked with the following words. *Rapu ya ka okwuo-okwu no mmadu ibe gi ka obu.* "Let him express himself for he is a human being like you". In short it is his humanity so to say that gives

---

[4] Uchendu V.C., *op. cit.*, p. 42.

[5] Uchendu V.C., *op. cit.*, p. 43.

him the right to freedom of expression and not other social considerations. Thus the Igbo express in practical way the concept that men have rights because they are human beings and not because the society confers these rights on them and man is endowed with these rights in order that he may fulfill himself as a social and spiritual being.

Igbo Laws and the Preservation of Rights

The system and principles of "Ohacracy" ensure that no laws which infringe on the fundamental rights of the citizens are enacted in Igbo country. All laws are intended for the common good and for the security of the collective rights of the people. This is made possible through the rigorous legislative processes which are open to all villagers without exception.

Laws are made from time to time regulating the use of and access to some common village assets like economic trees, land, reserved lakes and streams for fishing etc. in such a way that no individuals or group of individuals have monopoly of them. In other words, such laws are made to protect the individuals' rights to these bounties of nature and to check the excessive greed of the individuals who would trample upon others' rights in an effort to satisfy their selfish ends.[6]

It is the individual and collective obligation and responsibility of all Igbo, in pursuance of social justice and guided by their laws and customs not to stand by sequestered while somebody is being denied his rights on any grounds whatsoever. For instance if two person are fighting over a right to certain object, the first person who appears at the scene is obliged to stop the fight if he is strong enough to do so. Others who may come by the scene would join the peace-making. The persons fighting would be asked to state their cases. Whoever was guilty would be rebuked instantly. The disputed object would be restored to the rightful owner. And the aggressor reported to his family for further action. If the aggressor refuses to accept the verdict and the people intervening in the fight are satisfied that the aggressor is only asserting his right to the object because of his physical strength, he will be physically challenged by another fellow from among the mediators who is stronger that he is.

Whenever there is an infringement upon the individual right, any traditional Igbo of age who happens to be at the scene is obliged to condemn the violation of the right and use all means at is disposal to defend

---

[6] Cf. The law regulating the use of palm tree in Umuneke - chapter IV, p. 70 of this book.

the victim. The Igbo defending the right of others will go as much length as he would go in asserting his own. This has helped in the maintenance of justice and the preservation of individual rights.

The rule of law which is guaranteed by the Igbo "Ohacracy" is religiously observed in all Igbo communities. All Igbo are equal in right even though not in social status, and also equal before the law. The popular Igbo saying "*Igbo enwe eze*" ("the Igbo has no King") has double meaning. It means that the Igbo do not accept despotism or any form of authocracy. It also refers to the political and social attitude of the Igbo which is equal rights for all and special privileges for none (*Privi-legium* - outside the law). Thus the strict observance of the rule of law in Igbo communities eliminates all forms of class distinction.

To a large extent therefore, the Igbo positive laws play a significant role in the preservation of the rights of the villagers. At least the laws as we have seen previously do not infringe on the rights of the individuals and they are in all cases made for the common good of the people.

The Igbo Religion and Human Rights

In comparism with the Igbo laws, the Igbo natural religion plays a more vital role in the protection and preservation of the human rights in the native society. Most religions play this role as well.

The Igbo religion "*Ofoism*" is a non-aggressive and non-proselytising religion. It is concerned with the welfare of man here since the "hereafter" is more or less the continuation of life as it is on earth. For this reason, *Ofoism* is an indispensable factor of political control, social stability and cultural continuity.

By means of its doctrines, principles and values, the Igbo natural religion infuses into the Igbo high sense of moral discipline, a remarkable degree of tolerance and a deep respect for the feelings, interests and rights of all persons. Among others, the value placed on human life is note-worthy. The life of the individual is deemed sacred and is directly protected by *Ala*, the earth - goddess although "*Chukwu*" is the giver of life. For this reason, everything relating to the life of the individual is strictly regulated by "*Omenena*".[7]

Any direct interference with the life of any individual in the Igbo native society carries a religious sanction. Religious sanctions are much more dreaded by the Igbo than any form of social sanction, for the former may make him lose favour with the ancestors with the consequent denial of entry

---

[7] "*Omenana*" includes the religion, morality, laws and custom of the Igbo.

into *Ala muo* the happy abode of his forefathers or it may jeopardise his chances of reincarnation which is equally grave while the latter has only temporal social effects.

Homicide carries a serious religious sanction. It is a direct offence against *Ala*, a violation of the divine law and a flagrant infringement on the fundamental human right. Thus, the notorious Igbo who kills his fellow citizens by magic, sorcery, witchcraft or poisoning or other occult means would be expected to die a "bad death" and would be denied a ground burial which means that the gate to the ancestral abode is eternally shut against him.

Cold-blooded murder carries a "death penalty" - the murderer is expected, to hang himself. A purification rite is required to pacify the earth - goddess and to sweep off the ash of murder - (*Izafuntu ochu*). Every homicide is regarded as "polluting the land" desecracting the land. The murderer is believed to be haunted by the blood of his victim if he fled away from the community and he may never live a happy life both here and hereafter.

The high value placed on the life of the individual and the complex religious and social consequences of interfering with it either openly by violence or clandestinely by poisoning, sorcery etc. have engendered what tantamounts to a religious respect for the individual right to existence. It is therefore evident that the Igbo religion plays a vital role in the protection and preservation of the right to life, a right they consider as sacred and inalienable.

Over and above the effectiveness of its doctrine, principles and values in the protection of the human rights to life, the Igbo religion provides a safety for people whose lives are under serious threats. If a villager whose life is under a serious threat takes refuge at the shrine of the tutelar deity of the village, his safety is *ipso facto* assured. No person or group of persons dare to harm anyone who has taken refuge in the shrine. Even after he had left the shrine, nobody will bring harm on him on this religious conviction that the fellow has offered himself to the deity. By this act of seeking refuge in the shrine, the refugee obtains security but it is a boomerang. The refugee acquires a religious status but loses his social standing among the people.

During the inter-state wars in the later part of 17th century in Igbo country, many war prisoners regained their right to life by fleeing to the shrines. While some regained their freedom by voluntarily seeking refuge at the shrines, others obtained freedom by being offered to the service of a deity. The persons who have so been offered to the service of deity either voluntarily or otherwise are known as *Osu* in Igbo land. The *Osu* carries a social stigma and suffers a number of social disabilities. But paradoxically, these social disabilities are the sources of their ritual privilege and legal protection. Being under the custody of the deity they could not be sold,, killed or expropriated. On the other hand, the cult-slave status of the *Osu* stands as the greatest contradiction to the Igbo egalitarianism and seriously challenges the role of *Ofoism* in the protection and promotion of human rights. For the *Osu* are a people with a status dilemma, a people hated and despised yet indispensable in their ritual roles; a people whose achievements are spurned by a society which is aggressively achievement oriented. Although *Osu* function as "special" priests, they are not accorded the high status other priests who are "general practioners" enjoy. Rather the *Osu* are hated and feared, treated as if mean and discussed with the tone of horror and contempt".[8]

The "*Osu* caste" does not contradict the Igbo egalitarian ideology or philosophy of equal rights, nor the role of *Ofoism* in the area of human rights. The *Osu* caste must be seen as an isolated social reality which found rationalisation in Igbo religious belief. The *Osu* caste thrived only within a specific epoch of Igbo religious era.

It is therefore a past practice due to past ignorance. The cult-slave status was abolished by a legislation of the Eastern Nigerian Government in 1956. However the *Osu* system is not altogether dead.

The *Osu* and their descendants are still known and regarded as such. But at the present, they suffer no social disabilities except that the *Osu* and the non-*Osu* rarely inter-marry. The Igbo religion also plays a significant role in the protection of the individual's right to property. By regarding certain kinds of theft as taboo, *Nso*, the Igbo religion promotes the right to private property. Among others, the stealing of yam seedlings is an outright abomination. Yam is a very important crop in Igbo land. It is used as a measure of one's wealth. It is normally the target of every male traditional Igbo to have a full yam-barn since it is regarded as a mark of wealth and industry.

No wonder therefore why the stealing of yam seedlings carries a religious sanction. For to interfere with one's yam seedlings is to interfere with his most cherished property and the major source of his livelihood. This is nothing but an infringement on his fundamental right and the Igbo religion forbids it.

Apart from religious sanctions, the Igbo religious principles require the non-interference with other people's property. It is the Igbo religious creed

---

[8] Uchendu V.C. *op. cit.*, p. 89.

that one's property is an affair between him and his personal "*chi*". If he is not progressing economically or otherwise, he does but blames his "*chi*". In the light of this religious belief and principle, a typical Igbo is contented with what he has, little be it or much. He will say with contentment, "*Nkechinyelu*", the much my "*chi*" gives me is enough for me. In this way the religion curbs that excessive greed which leads men to interfere with what belongs to others.

A typical Igbo seeks redress by appealing to a powerful deity or to an oracle when his property is secretly taken away or unjustly appropriated by another. If secretly taken away, he would invoke the deity or the oracle as the case may be to punish the doers. Unjustly appropriated, he would insist that the claimant should swear on any deity of his choice. The Igbo believes that the deity will vindicate his right by punishing the man who has so unjustly acquired another person's property.

The native Igbo strongly believes that if the deity is invoked against the person or persons who have another person's property, the deity will punish not only the thieves but all who may partake of the stolen goods. Because of this religious belief if a person is ill he or she may start wondering whether his illness is not caused by his having unknowingly partaken of stolen goods. In case of serious doubt, he may consult a diviner. As for swearing falsely in order to acquire another persons' property the consequences are far-reaching. These religious beliefs and practices make the Igbo respect the property of others. Thus, in this way albeit indirectly the Igbo religion promotes and protects the right of the individual to private property.

The social doctrine of *Ofoism* is summarised in the following words which the *Ofoist* often utters while breaking a kola-nut or in his evening or morning prayers:

"*Egbe belu, ugo belu, nke si ibe ya ebena, nku ka ya.*" Literally this can be rendered as, "Let the kite perch and let the eagle perch too, whichever prevents the other from perching let its wings break". It is a doctrine of peaceful coexistence based on the philosophy of equal rights. The above dictum needs further analysis for it is pregnant with meaning.

Egbe the Kite and *Ugo* the eagle are all birds but with different characteristics and physical features. Their common abode is the *Orji*, Iroko tree (*chlorophora excelsa*). *Egbe* has to perch on the *Orji* and *Ugo* has to perch on it too. But if either of them refuses to allow the other perch on the tree, let it lose its right to that abode.

The native Igbo is noted for expressing important ideas in proverbial language. The Kite and the Eagle situation refers to the actual human situation in the society with warring interests.

Iroko, represents the earth at large with the communities of men. Now, "the doctrine of *Ofoism*" charges all men to live in peaceful coexistence in their communities despite personal interests by mutual respect of each other's right to the earthly abode and nature's bounties. Then the sanction follows: whoever should interfere with other's right to the common earthly abode and nature's bounties should himself lose the right to the same.

In the above terse but lucid proverbial statement of value, the social doctrine of the Igbo religion is encapsuled. In essence, the doctrine sets out to state the principles which if adhered to will promote social justice and foster social harmony and political stability. For a peaceful coexistence among men to be possible which is essentially the injuction of *Ofoism*, men must learn not to interfere with people's rights and liberty.

It is clearly evident from the foregoing that the Igbo religion plays an indispensable role in the protection and preservation of human rights of the Igbo people. *Ofo*ism is a religion with social mission and without it the Igbo political and social instiutions would fall asunder. An Igbo Political scientist Njaka rightly remarked:

"As in other nations and states, religion has been one of the dominant forces molding the Igbo country and it continues to generate the doctrines, principles, and values which characterise the Igbo polity".[9]

Emerging from our whole discussion are the facts that the Igbo positive laws are designed to safeguard the rights of the people; that tyrannical laws which do violate to human rights are not enactable following the singular legislative processes of the Igbo "Ohacracy"; that the Igbo religion, by means of its doctrines, principles and values plays a more effective role than the laws in protecting and preserving the individual rights in the Igbo society and that *Ofoism* remains the centripetal force that weld the political, social and religious lives of the Igbo together into a harmonious whole.

---

[9] Njaka, E.N., *Igbo Political Culture*, *op. cit.*, p. 49.

Conclusion

A Challenge To Legal Positivism.

The Igbo positive laws, together with their legislative and judicial methods which as we have seen are inseparably bound with their religion and morality stand as a challenge to legal positivism.

By legal positivism, we mean essentially that attitude of mind and spirit which regard as valid laws only such enforceable norms formally enacted or established by the appropriate official political organ.

In the legal positivist's view, only municipal laws or statute laws are laws indeed, for they have been formally so posited by the authority. A given norm or proposal, having formally and successfully passed through the technical procedure of legislation, acquires *ipso facto*, the force of law regardless of all other considerations - moral, teleological and practical. This is the view and stance of legal positivism and its protagonists.

The legal positivist' is not in any way bothered by what the law ought to be. Right or wrong, it does not really matter so long as the law bears the stamp of authority. Thus, it is the formal stamp of technical legality on a given norm and not its ethical content or moral soundness that is the criterion of legal validity. It is thus clear that legal positivism separates ethics from jurisprudence, divorces morality from positive law and makes the will of the legislative organ the only Source of law, as it severes the legal "is" from the legal "ought".

Since the state or legislative authority is the only recognised sources of law in the legal positivist view, and its will the law itself, any further criterion such as the inherent justice or the moral lawfulness of the action prescribed by the law becomes irrelevant. If political sovereignty is the only legitimate source of valid laws, there is no doubt that customary law, canon law, positive international law as well as other legitimate legal phenomena are in serious danger.[1]

The legal phenomena in the Igbo country are opposed to the spirit and tenet of legal positivism. For instance, in theory and in practice the Igbo does not conceive law as separate from morality. Laws in the Igbo traditional setting must conform with the ethics and morality of the people. This means that a piece of legislation does not necessarily become a law

---

[1] Cf. *"Right and Laws in Thomas Hobbes' Ethical and Political Theory"*, (A Master's thesis submitted by me), Urban University Rome, 1980, pp. 84-86.

simply because the proposed legislation has passed through the legislative technicalities successfully.

For a piece of legislation to qualify as law in the Igbo traditional setting such a piece of legislation must be seen as morally right and just and of course must be known as proceeding from the will of the people.

Our indigenous law - makers on whom the responsibility of making laws that affect the lives of a wider community in our developing nation rests would be doing the society a great service if they make laws that are consistent with the spirit and values of our traditional jurisprudence.

By the same token, our indigenous judges must guard against the inroads of the aberration of legal positivism that invaded, beguiled and seduced the minds of many western jurists. For there is a great fear that most of our indigenous "modern" judges are under the spell of western legal influences with the consequent danger of their insisting on the separation of morality from positive laws in our land. A. Soras has warned that:

> Such a separation of morality and positive law threatens more largely today because so many contemporary jurists, especially among the Anglo - saxons, are empiricists.[2]

Legal positivists erred not only in their separation of morality from positive laws but also in their claim that the sovereign or a constituted legislative authority is the only source of valid laws. This claim would be considered a legal heresy in Igbo jurisprudence. In the first place, the Igbo have no sovereigns as such and need neither emperors nor empires.

They have no standing constituted legislative authority as such either. The people themselves, the "Oha" are the sovereign authority and the legislative authority rests on them. With the sovereign authority invested on the "Oha" and the legislative powers entrusted on no special group to the exclusion of other groups, the dangers of legal authoritarianism and tyranny are forestalled and eliminated. On the other hand, the legal climate created by legal positivism is favourable for the enactment of oppressive and tyrannical laws. Here again, the legal phenomena in Igbo land stand as a living contradiction to the spirit and tenet of legal positivism.

Furthermore, enforceability is an essential element in the positivist's definition of law. For according to legal positivism, only such *enforceable* norms formally enacted by the appropriate official political organ or the state are valid laws. This means that laws must be backed by a coercive force. The contrary is the case in the Igbo traditional legal setting.

---

2 Soras, A., *International Morality*, Burn & Oates, London, 1963, p. 18.

The Igbo positive laws, because of their religious and moral import, bind the individuals in conscience - *in foro interno*. Sanctions rather than force applied to ensure obedience to the laws. And this is why the Igbo had no real need for a standing law enforcement agents. Uchendu has rightly described the Igbo system as:

> a government in which the use of force is minimal or absent....[3]

The task before our law-makers today is to study more critically our indigenous institutions, especially the legal institutions with a view to rediscovering those good values inherent in our traditional legal system. These values should not be allowed to fall into oblivion in the face of the rising tide of legal positivism in our land.

Furthermore, in respect of the consciences and aspirations of the people, our "modern" law - makers and judges should resist the urge to design laws divorced from our philosophy, from the nature of beings, as we understand them, and from our view of the world.

In this regard, I commend the efforts of some of our law - makers in the National Assembly. Quite recently, an abortion Bill tabled before the National Assembly for the purpose of legislation into law was unable to sail through the assembly. This Bill, if passed into law, would have made abortion legal in our nation.

Following a wide and wild public reaction in protest to the Bill, and aware of the social and moral impact of such a legislation, the law - makers dropped the abortion Bill and it did not become law. To have legalised abortion in blind imitation of the western nations and contrary to our traditional values and views, would have given rise to serious moral tensions among the peoples of our nation.

But the dangers are not over. This is why there is need for dialogue between the "traditionalists" and the so - called "modernists". The need for a further research into the relative merits of our indigenous institutions as a whole is even now more pressing. And I believe that my philosophical inquiry into the nature of laws and rights in the traditional Igbo society is a valuable contribution to this end.

---

[3] Uchendu, V.C., op. cit. p. 46

Postscript

British Influence On Igbo Judicial Methods

Under British Colonial Administration, which dated back from the beginning of this century, the judicial system described has undergone some changes. For administrative reasons, the British Colonial Government established courts by the Native Courts Proclamation in 1900. Following the Proclamation, Igboland was arbitrarily carved into Native Courts Areas, created by grouping a number of neighbouring village-groups which were traditionally sovereign political units. Each Court Area constituted a native court system, an all-purpose administrative machinery. The British District Commissioner was the president of the court, with warrant chiefs, court clerks and messengers as personnel. The warrant chiefs who were given caps of office and a warrants of authority which were backed by the coercive force of the administration were individuals chosen by the British with no particular reference to their position in the native society. The system was therefore doomed to failure and it actually failed.

The famous Aba riots of 1929-30 was infact a revolt against taxation and against the warrant chiefs together with discontentment at the low price of palm oil. Following the bloody riot which took place in the heart of Igboland and claimed several lives, more and more intelligence reports were demanded from government officials on the subject of the traditional or rather the "natural rulers" of the Igbo. The reform of 1930-1931 that followed attempted to correct the ills of the old system. The new native courts which came with the indirect rule were adapted to the existing native institutions. The old "Court Area" was re-delineated into small zones thereby reflecting the nature of the social groupings. The number of benches and judgeships were accordingly increased. Individuals no longer held "Warrants" but social units ie villages. The villages selected court judges to represent them. In actual practice, it was the holder of the big *Ọfọ* from each village who was chosen as court member. This Reform gave the British established courts a native outlook.

Other Native Courts reforms under British Colonial Administration are:

I) The 1918 Reform, in which the Native Court Ordinance (No. 5 as amended to 1922) abolished the office of district commissioner in the native courts and thus made the courts really native. (Nevertheless this reform created many other problems);

II) The 1956 Reform which replaced the name "Native Court" with "Customary Court".

The definition of customary law was provided in S.2 of the Customary Courts Law, 1956, of the Eastern Region and reads:

> In this law... "Customary law" means a rule or body of rules regulating rights and imposing correlative duties, being a rule or body of rules which obtains and is fortified by established usage and which is appropriate and applicable to any particular matter, dispute, issue or question.[1]

Thus, the Customary Court was empowered to administer indigenous law and custom (in so far as they are not repugnant to "natural justice") and has power within its own sphere of competence to enforce its decisions. Section 13 of the Eastern Nigeria High Court law, 1955 (as amended) states:

> Except in so far as the Governor may by order otherwise direct and except in suits transferred to the High Court under the provisions of the Native Courts Ordinance or the Customary Courts law, 1956, the Court shall not exercise original jurisdiction in any cause or matter which is subject to the jurisdiction of a Native Court or Customary Court....[2]

It is clear that the Customary Courts have complete jurisdiction over matters of purely customary nature.

Neither the "Native Court" as amended nor the "Customary Court" could replace effectively the traditional judicial system already discussed. That the Native Court of British creation has considerable impact on Igbo traditional judicial institution no one disputes. The indigenous judicial institution nonetheless survived till today. Nowadays, however, an injured party, in addition to these indigenous methods, may avail himself of the Local Customary Courts.

Green, who completed a case study of Umuneke village in the heart of Igboland, writing about the British established Courts says:

> The Court was there: but in point of fact the people of Umuneke did not use it. In all the time that I was in the village I only heard of one case taken to it... Much later in my stay I found that this absentation from the court was at least in part a conscious and, so to speak, official policy on the part of the village.[3]

What Green observed about Umuneke's attitude towards the court is true of most villages in Igboland. At any event, the indigenous judicial methods still exists vis - a - vis the courts.

---

[1] Section 2 of the Customary Courts Law, 1956, of the Eastern Region of Nigeria.

[2] Section 13 of the Eastern Region Enactment.

[3] Green, M.M. *op. cit.* p. 103.

Bibliography

Sources On Igbo People

Books

Achebe, C.,	*The Arrow of God*, London, Heinemann Press, 1967.
————	*Things Fall Apart*, London, Heinemann Press, 1969.
Arinze, F. A.,	*Sacrifice In Igbo Religion*, Ibadan, University Press, 1970.
Anochie, R. C.,	*The Impact of Igbo Women On the Church in Igboland*, Rome, 1979.
Arderner, E.,	*Lineage and Locality Among the Mbaise Ibos in Africa*, London 1959.
Basden, G. T.,	*Among the Ibos of Nigeria*, London, Frank Cass & Co. Ltd., 1966.
Basden, G.T	*Niger Ibos*, London, Frank Cass & Co. Ltd., 1971.
Ekechi, F.K.	*Missionary Enterprise and Rivalry in Igbo Land*, London, Frank Cass & Co. Ltd., 1971.
Ekezie, J.O.,	*Spiritual Renaissance In Nigeria*, Nsukka, 1970.
Elias, T.O.,	*Nigeria Land Law and Custom*, London, Routledge and Kegan Paul Ltd., 1954.
Elias, T.O.,	*The Nature of African Customary Law*, Manchester, University Press, 1956.
Elias, T.O.,	*The Nigerian Legal System*, Routledge and Kegan Ltd., London, 1964.
Ford, D. & Jones, G.,	*The Ibo and Ibibio Speaking Peoples of South-Eastern Nigeria*, London, International Institute, 1967.
Forsyth, F.,	*The Making of an African Legend: The Biafrian Story*, Penguin Books, 1977.
Green, M.N.,	*Igbo Village Affairs*, London, Frank Cass & Co. Ltd., 1969.
Hailey, F.	*Native Administration in the The British African Territories*, 5 Vols., London, 1951.
Henderson, R.N.	*The King in Every Man, Evolutionary Trends in Onitsha Society and Culture*, New Haven & London, 1972.
Harris, P.T.	*Local Government In Southern Nigeria*, Cambridge University Press, 1957.
Ilogu, E.,	*Christianity and the Igbo Culture*, Leiden, e.j. Brill, 1974.

Isichei, E.,   *The Ibo People and the Europeans,* London, Faber & Faber Ltd., 1971.

Isichei, E.,   *The History of Ibo People*, London, The Macmillan Press Ltd. 1976.

Isichei, E.,   *The Igbo Worlds*, Macmillan Educational Ltd., London, 1977.

Leith-Ross, S.,   *Beyond the Niger*, London, Lutterworth Press, 1951.

Leith-Ross, S.,   *African Women: A Study of the Ibo of Nigeria*, London, Routledge & Kegan Paul, Ltd., 1965.

Njaka, E.N.,   *Igbo Political Culture*, Evanston, Northwestern University Press, 1974.

Nsugbe, P.O.,   *A Matrilineal Ibo People*, Oxford, The Clarendon Press, 1974.

Nwala, T.U.,   Igbo Philosopy, Lagos, Literamed Publication, 1985.

Nwankwo, A.A.   *Nigeria: The Challenge of Biafra*, Rex Collins, London, 1972.

Nzimiro, F.I.,   *Family and Kinship in Ibo Land*, Cologne, 1962.

Nzimiro, F.I.   *Studies in Igbo Political Systems, Chieftaincy and Politics in Four Niger States*, University of California Press, 1972.

O'donnell, N.,   *Religion and Morality among the Ibo of Southern Nigeria*, London, 1937.

Ogbalu, F.C.,   *Igbo Institutions and Customs*, Onitsha,University Publishing Press (not dated).

Ogbalu, F.C.,   *Ilu Igbo (The Book of Igbo Proverbs)*, University Publishing Company, Onitsha, 2nd ed. 1965.

Okafor-Omali, D.,   *A Nigerian Village in two Worlds*, London, Faber & Faber Limited, 1965.

Perham, M.,   *Native Administration in Nigeria*, London, 1937.

Smock, A.,   *Ibo Politics, The Role of Ethnic Unions in Eastern Nigeria*, Cambridge, Mass., 1971.

Talbot, P. A.,   *Tribes on the Niger Delta*, London, The Sheldom Press, 1937.

Uchendu, V. C.,   *The Igbo of South-Eastern Nigeria*, London, Holt, Rinehart & Winston, 1965.

Articles:

Anene, J. C.,   *The Southern Protectorate and the Aros*, 1900-1902, J.H.S.N., I/I/1956.

Armstrong, R. G.,   *The Development of Kingdoms in Negro Africa*, J.H.S.N., II/I/1960.

Boston, J.,   *Notes on the Origin of the Igala Kingship*, J.H.S.N., II/3/1962.

Igbo, E. O.,   *Conflicts Between Traditional Religion and Christianity in Igboland, South-Eastern Nigeria*, West African Religion, N. 10. Nsukka - Nigeria: Department of Religion, University of Nigeria, 1971.

Hambly, W.D.,   *Culture Areas of Nigeria*, Chicago, Field Museum of Natural History (Anthropological Series XXXI, 3), 1953.

Hountondji, P.,   *African Philosophy, Myth and Reality*, Thought and Practice 1/2, 1974.

Hunnings, G.,   *Logic, Language and Culture*, a paper read at the Nigerian Philosophical Association Conference, University of Ife, Nigeria, 1975.

Iwuagwu, A. O.,   *Chukwu: Towards a Definition*, West African Religion, NO. 10 (not dated).

Igbafe, P. A.,   *Western Ibo Society and its Resistance to British Rule*, journal of African History, XII, 1971.

Jones, G. I.,   *The Jones Report: Report on the Status of Chiefs*, Eastern Nigeria, Government Printer, Enugu, Nigeria, 1956.

Kalu, O. U.,   *Gods in Retreat: Models of Religious change in Africa*, Nigerian Journal of the Humanities, I/I Sept. 1977.

———————   *Missionaries, Colonial Government and Secret Societies in South-Eastern Igboland, 1900-1950*. Journal of the Historical Society of Nigeria, 9, 1978.

O'Donohue, J.,   *African Philosophy: The Problem of Definition*, a paper read at the Nigerian Philosophical Association Conference, University of Ife, Nigeria, 1975.

Okere, T.,   *The Relation Between Culture and Philosophy, Uche: Journal of the Department of Philosophy*, University of Nigeria, Nsukka, 2, 1976.

Onyewuenyi, I.,   *Is There An African Philosophy?*, Journal of African Studies, III/4 Winter, 1976.

Ottenberg, S.,   *Ibo Oracles and Inter-group Relations*, Southwestern
                      Journal of Anthropology, Vol. 14, 1958.

————————   *Ibo Receptivity to Change, Continuity and Change in
                      African Cultures*, W.J. Bascom And M.J. Herskovits
                      (eds), Chicago: University of Chicago Press, Phoenix
                      Edition, 1962.

————————   *Local Government and Law in Southern Nigeria*,
                      Journal of Asian and African Studies, II, 1967.

Perry, R.,   *New Sources for Research in Nigerian History*, Africa,
                      XXV, 3, 1955.

Thomas, N. W.,   *Anthropological Report on the Ibo-Speaking Peoples of
                      Nigeria*, Part I, Law and Custom of the Ibo of the
                      Awka Neigbourhood, London, 1913.

————————   *Anthropological Report on the Ibo-Speaking Peoples of
                      Nigeria*, Part IV, Law and Custom of the Asaba
                      District, London, 1914.

Wieschoff, H. A.,   *Social Significance of Names among the Ibo of
                      Nigeria*, American Anthropologist, Vol. 43, 1941.

Sources On African Life
Books:

Ainslie, P.,   *The Press in Africa: Communication Past and Present*,
                      London, Victor Collenz Ltd., 1962.

Ajayi, J. F. A.,   *Christian Missions in Nigeria*, 1841-1891, Longman,
                      1965.

Annene, B.,   *Africa in the Nineteenth and Twentieth Centuries*,
                      Nigeria, Ibadan University Press, 1970.

Ayandele, E. A.,   *The Political and Social Implication of Missionary
                      `Enterprise in the Evolution of Modern Nigeria*,
                      Unpublished Ph. D. Thesis, University of London,
                      1964.

Bachanan, K. M.
& Pugh, J. C.,   *Land and People in Nigeria*, London, 1955.

Brry, Bronowski,   *Growth of Ideas, Knowledge Thought Imagination*,
VVV,   London, Adus book Ltd., 1965.

Bascom, W. R. &
Herskovits, M. J.,   *Continuity and Change in African Culture*, Chicago,
                      1965.

Blyden, E. W.,   *African life and Custom*, London, African Publication
                      Society, 1969.

Bohannan, P. J.,   *Justice and Judgment among the Tiv*, London, 1955.

Brokensha, D., & Crowder, M.,	*Africa in The Wider World, The Inter-relationship of Area and Comparative Studies,* Pergamon Press Ltd., Oxford, 1967.
Buell, R. L.,	*The Native Problem in Africa,* 2 Vols. New York, 1928.
Cameron, D.,	*Principles of Native Administration and their Application,* Lagos, 1934.
Cole, P.,	*Modern and Traditional Elites in the Politics of Lagos,* Cambridge, Cambridge University Press, 1975.
Cornford, F. M.,	*From Religion to Philosophy,* New York, 1957.
Cowan, L. G.,	*Local Government in West Africa,* New York, 1958.
Crocker, W. R.,	*Nigeria: A Critique of British Colonial Administration,* London, 1936.
Crowder, M.,	*The Story of Nigeria,* London, Faber and Faber, 4th ed. 1976.
Davidson, B.,	*Old Africa Rediscovered,* London, 1959.
Dike, K. O.,	*Trade and Politics in the Niger Delta,* 1830-1855, London, 1956.
————	*100 years of British Rule in Nigeria, 1851-1951,* Lagos, 1957.
Elias, T. O.,	*Government and Politics in Africa,* London, Asia Publishing House Bombay, 2nd ed. 1963.
Ezera, K.,	*Constitutional Developments in Africa,* London, 1960.
Finnegan, R.,	*Oral literature in Africa,* Oxford Clarendon Press, 1970.
Fortes, M.,	Evans-Pritchard, E., *African Political System,* London, 1940.
Hailey, F.,	*Native Administration in the British African Territories,* 5 vols., London, 1951.
Hodgkin, T.,	*African Political Parties,* London, Penguin, 1961.
————	*Nationalism in Colonial Africa,* New York, University Press, 1965.
Idowu, E. B.,	*African Traditional Religion,* London, S.C.M. Press Ltd., 1974.
Kwasi, W.,	*Philosophy and an African Culture,* Cambridge University Press, 1980.
Langa, L.,	*Up Against it in Nigeria,* London, 1922.
Lerner, D.,	*The Passing of Traditional Society,* New York, The free Press, 1958.

Maguet, J.,	*Power and Society in Africa*, New York, Magraw Hill Book Co., 1971.
Mair, L. P.,	*Native Policies in Africa*, London, 1936.
Mbiti, J. S.,	*African Religions and Philosophy*, London, Heinemann Educational Books, Ltd., 1971.
Meddleton, J.,	*Black Africa: Its Peoples and their Customs Today*, London, Micmillan Co., 1970
Meek, C. K.,	*Northern Tribes of Nigeria*, London, 1925.
Mockler-Ferryman, A. F.,	*British Nigeria*, London, 1902.
Morez, E. D.,	*Nigeria, Its Peoples and Problems*, 2nd ed. London, 1912.
Nduka O.,	*Western Education and The Nigerian Cultural Background*, London, Oxford University Press, 1975.
Niven, C. R.,	*A Short History of the Yoruba Peoples*, London, 1958.
Nwabueze, B. O.,	*The Machinery of Justice in Nigeria*, London, Butterworth Co. (Publishers) Ltd., 1963.
Onwuejeogwu, M. A.,	*The Social Anthropology of Africa*, London, Heinemann, 1975.
Parrinder, G.,	*Africa's Three Religions*, Sheldom Press, London, 1976.
Perham, M.,	*Native Administration in Nigeria*, London, 1937.
Shorter, A.,	*African Culture and the Christian Church*, An Introduction to Social and Pastoral Anthropology, London, Geoffrey Chapman, 1973.
Soras, A.,	*International Morality*, London, Burns & Oates, 1963.
Talbot, P. A.,	*The People of Southern Nigeria*, Vol. 1, Oxford, 1926.
Tamuno, T. N.,	*Nigeria and Elective Representative 1923-1947*, London, Heinemann, 1966.
Taylor, E. B.,	*Primitive Culture*, London, 1871.
Wheare, J.,	*The Nigerian Legislative Council*, London, 1950.

Sources On Philosophy Of Law

Aquinas, T., — *Treatise on Law (Summa Theologica, Questions 90-97),* Introduction by Parry, S., Gateway Editions Ltd., South Bend, Indiana, 1976.

Austin, J., — *The Providence of Jurisprudence Determined,* London, 1832.

Benn, S. I., & Peters, R. S., — *Social Principles and the Democratic State,* London, 1959. Reissued as *Principles of Political Thought,* New York, 1964.

Bosanquet, B., — *Philosophical Theory of the State,* 1899, 4th ed., London, 1923.

Composta, D., — *Natura e Ragione, Studio Sulle inclinazioni naturali in rapporto al diritto naturale,* Zurich, Pas-Verlag, 1971.

Cranston, M. W. — *What Are Human Rights?* New York, 1963. Preface by Reinhold Niebuhr.

Davitt, T. E., — *Law as a Means to an End,* Thomas Aquinas (1960-1961) 14 Vanderbilt Law Review, 65.

Delvin, P., — *The Enforcement of Morals,* London, Oxford University Press, 1965.

D'Entreves, A. P. — *Natural Law, An Introduction to Legal philosophy,* Huntchinson, 2nd ed., 1970.

Dias, R. W. M., — *A Bibliography of Jurisprudence,* London, 1964.

Dworkin, R. M., — *The Philosophy of Law,* Oxford, University Press, 1977.

Frankena, W. K., — *Natural and Inalienable Rights.* Philosophical Review, Vol. 64 (1955), 212-232.

Hagerstom, A., — *Inquiries Into the Nature of Law and Morals,* translated by C. D. Broad; Karl Olivecrona, ed. Stockholm, 1953.

Hart, H. L. A., — *The Concept of Law,* Oxford, Clarendon Press, 1961.

————— *Law, Liberty and Morality,* London, Oxford University Press, 1966.

Hegel, — *Hegel's Philosophy of Rights* (translated with notes by T. M. Knox) London, Oxford University Press, 1978.

Iwe, N. S. S., — *Human Rights in History and Documents,* Rome, Lateran University Press, 1969.

Kelsen, H.,   *General Theory of Law and State* (20th Century Legal Philosophy Series Vol. I) Russel, New York, 1961.

Maritain, J.,   *Les Droits de l'homme et la loi naturelle*, New York, 1942. Translated by Doris, C. A., as *The Rights of Man and Natural Law*, New York, 1943.

Meld, A. I.,   *Rights and Right Conducts*, Oxford, 1927.

Messner, J.,   *Social Ethics-Natural Law in the Modern World*, London, Herder Book Co., 1957.

milchell, B.,   *Law, Morality and Religion in a Secular Society*, London, Oxford University Press, 1967.

Pizzorni, R. M.,   *Attualita del diritto naturale?* Roma, Liberia Editrice, 1971.

—————   *Il diritto naturale dalle origini a S. Tommaso D'Aquino*, Roma Citta Nuova Editrice, 1978.

Pollock, B.,   *Essay on Jurisprudence and Ethics*, London, 1956.

Pound, R.,   *Law and Morals*, New York, A. M. Kelly Publishers, 1969.

Rommen, H. A.,   *The Natural Law - A Study in Legal and Social History and Philosophy*, London, Herder Book Co., 1959.

Other Sources

Alpern, H.,   *The March of Philosophy*, New York, 1934.

Blanchette, A.,   *The Philosophy of Psychoanalysis*, Ottawa, 1946.

Collins, J.,   *Readings in Ancient and Medieval Philosophy.* (Selected introduction and commentary). The College Reading series 6, Westminister, Newman Press, 1960.

Gleen, P. I.,   *Cosmology, A Class Manual in the Philosophy of Bodily Being*, London, B. Herder Book Co., 1949.

Misch, G.,   *The Dawn of Philosophy*, London, 1950.

Nikam , N. A.,   *Science and Philosophy: Individual Freedom and Community, Traditional Values*, Mysore, Wesley Press, 1959.

Robb, J. H.,   *Man as Infinite Spirit*, Milivankee, Marquette University Publication, 1974.

Smith, E.,   *African Ideas of God*, London, 1950.

Smith, C.,   *Sensism, The Philosophy of the West* New York, The Truth Seeker Co., 1956.

Temples, P.,   *Bantu Philosophy*, Paris, Presence Africaine, 1969.

Vycinas, V.,   *Greatness and Philosophy: An Inquiry into Western Thought,* The Hague, Nijhoff, 1966.

Wheelwright,   *The Way of Philosophy,* New York, The Odyssey Press, 1960.

Igbo Philosophy of Law
Index

---

[18] Njaka, E. N., *op. cit.*, p. 46.